MW00588459

Praise for *Dancing with a*

"A moving story about a teenager who got wrapped up in the emotional struggles of depression, anorexia and a life that moved too fast, and a mother who loved her daughter enough to let go and live. Together, their personal stories, journals and love letters navigate the reader through their struggle to understand the mental health treatment system, find emotional support, feel better and live life with gusto after surviving the consequences of an eating disorder. A must read!"

— Priscilla Wade, Ph.D., Psychologist

"Such a compelling journey of a mother's love and a daughter's recovery! This book will impact anyone who loves someone struggling with an eating disorder. There's nothing like hearing another's story to help you know you're not the only one who feels like the only one."

— Bethany Ginn Waldrop, LCSW, Eating Disorder Specialist

"Parents and loved ones of those with an eating disorder can find much information, hope and understanding in Ms. Foster's book, but above all, they can find that they are not alone. Ms. Foster details her anguish through Jenna's sudden sickness, her weight loss, her hospitalizations ... From questioning oneself, to negotiating treatments, to feeling helpless, to realizing the importance of self-care, Ms. Foster handled the challenges with exquisite love and dedication to her daughter. Her book is going to be a valuable resource for parents and loved ones of people with eating disorders."

— Erla Leon, Ph.D. Assistant Clinical Director, Shoreline Center for Eating Disorder Treatment - Satori House

"A unique story of mother and daughter struggling through the ravages of anorexia nervosa. From their combined journals, the engaging narrative provides an intimate understanding of the dynamics of a difficult social and psychological problem. Readers will gain considerable insight. Having practiced in Phoenix for twenty years treating eating disorders, I can highly recommend this book."

— Dr. Gregory Archer, Psychologist and author of *Private Heller and the Bantam Boys*

Also by Valerie Foster

The Risk of Sorrow:
Conversations with Holocaust Survivor,
Helen Handler

Dancing with a Demon

Valerie Foster

with

Jenna Warnecke

Albion Andalus
Boulder, Colorado
2017

"The old shall be renewed,

and the new shall be made holy."

— Rabbi Avraham Yitzhak Kook

Albion-Andalus, Inc.
P. O. Box 19852
Boulder, CO 80308
www.albionandalus.com

Design and layout by Samantha Krezinski

Cover design by Sari Wisenthal-Shore

Artwork by Jenna Warnecke

Photos courtesy of Tom Foster.

ISBN-13: 978-0692809365 (Albion-Andalus Books)

ISBN-10: 0692809368

To Jenna-Marie

and to the mothers who know

"Making the decision to have a child...
is to decide forever to have your heart
go walking around outside your body."
— Elizabeth Stone

"At the bottom of the abyss comes the voice
of salvation. The black moment is the moment
when the real message of transformation is going
to come. At the darkest comes the light."
— Joseph Campbell

Table of Contents

Prologue

A writer writes to two people—the one who says, "Oh, so that's how it is," and the one who says, "Ah yes, that's how it is."

I am afraid to remember; I am more afraid to forget. I am afraid to flippantly reminisce much later out of a soft complacency—afraid that if I forget the demon, it will quietly creep up and strike again. And so I write.

My daughter at seventeen years and seven months was a petite five feet, four inches tall, with chestnut brown hair, large brown eyes, long dark eyelashes, and creamy fair skin. She was in the eleventh grade, had a large circle of wonderful friends and a tight-knit clan of five close ones. She earned top grades, belonged to the drama club, was learning how to swing dance, and went to the Christmas semi-formal.

At seventeen and seven, Jenna wrote poetry, massaged her mom's feet at night, loved to share Frappucinos with her parents on the deck in the evenings while discussing philosophy or literature, and was discovering coffee houses.

Jenna spent every other weekend with her dad and was his fishing queen. She dearly loved her new stepdad and what he brought to her mother's life and the family's. "I couldn't imagine a better stepdad," she would often say. As feminine filling between two brothers, she learned much from each, got annoyed by each, and wouldn't trade either for the world. From Nathan, nineteen, she was learning about what college was really like. With Greg, thirteen, she had found a kindred spirit in a love of filmmaking.

At seventeen and seven, Jenna had had lessons in swimming, dancing, and playing the violin. She was in choir, on her school's swim team, and wrote in her journal. She went to church regularly and never squandered money, didn't drink, smoke, or do drugs. In her young life, Jenna had already traveled to New York City, Las Vegas, San Diego, Los Angeles, Colorado, the Grand Canyon, and Mexico.

By seventeen and seven, Jenna had a style all her own and was growing out her bangs. I never needed to dictate the clothes she wore because she always showed good sense, and we two actually enjoyed trips to the mall together. She didn't fall for the latest mad diets, wasn't boy-crazy, and was definitely not a trend or status-seeker.

Jenna and I enjoyed a close bond; she told me of her first kiss, discussed boys, philosophy, love, and life.

At seventeen years and seven months, my daughter was mature, sensible, creative, adventurous, independent, dynamic, poetic, cheerful, smart, lovely, and loving.

At seventeen years and eight months, Jenna stopped eating.

Jenna's Journal

My hands once contained
my life.
They held the key
to all I held
sacred.
They closed tightly
into a fist
around my talent,
my heart,
my life.
I thought they'd hold it all forever.
But one day
for a reason
I'll never understand
they
let
go.
And I fell apart.

Chapter One

One Hundred, Twenty-Nine Pounds

Shhhh, quiet. Be very quiet, for a powerful, evil monster just slid into our home, and we mustn't let him find us. Be quiet and still, and maybe he will go away, unsatisfied.

"Mom, can Carrie and Renee and I stop at the house after school while you guys are having the final walk-through? They want to see the house and I can't wait to show them!" My daughter's eyes twinkled with adolescent expectancy.

"Sure, hon. We'll be there about three o'clock, just when you get out of school."

Maybe that's when he slipped in. With the realtor, or the detail crew, or the movers, or us. Maybe he was built into the house somehow, or lay beneath the surface of the earth itself, waiting.

Our recently-blended family was on its way to settling into our new dynamics. Finally. Although my husband, Tom, and I had been married for eighteen months, this was the first point where our family of five was to live together under the same roof. Ours had been an unconventional merger, but then, "unconventional" has always described this magical relationship.

Six years earlier, as a divorced mother of three, I had found myself drawn to a most remarkable man. Tom and I were colleagues and friends teaching at the same high school, and after I transferred to a new school and watched my thirteen-year marriage dissolve, he and I began to date.

"Stay away from him, Valerie. He is an eternal bachelor. He's never been married, never even lived with anyone, and he runs from commitment. There's no way he'll take on three kids, either." Such were the words of my well-intentioned friends.

Well, I wasn't looking for marriage, so there. We dated off and on for five years and allowed our love to germinate at its own pace until we could not bear to be apart any longer. Jenna, Nate, and Greg had grown to love Tom and honor his place in our family, not in replacing their father, but in simply adding to their lives, especially as they watched how happy he made me. Unconventional romance culminated in an unconventional wedding, and three days before Thanksgiving of 1996, I sat down with my daughter and told her of our plans to elope to Carmel over the holiday weekend. When I reassured her we would have a repeat family ceremony soon after in which she would play an important role standing beside me, she smiled and gave us her heartfelt blessing. One month later came a second ceremony, a repeat of our vows among family and friends. Jenna was my attendant, and mother and daughter stood together, I dressed in black velvet, holding a calla lily, she in red velvet with a red rose.

When we all returned from a family honeymoon, we still had not begun living together. Once my house sold and we began construction on our dream home, we rented two apartments. One on the second floor for Tom, Greg, and me, and another below for Nate and Jenna. For the remaining ten months of construction this is how we lived. Through all our family's moves and changes, my children stayed grounded somehow, and as our closing date kept getting set back, Jenna kept her usual positive energy permeating whatever space we occupied. More than anyone, she modeled patience and optimism. "The house will be awesome, Mom. It's cool living in our own little apartment, Nate and me, and we'll be moving in, finally all together, before we know it. Everything's working out great!"

So now, at last it was moving day. Our two-story house had four bedrooms and enough areas for everyone to have personal space. All I could think of was how the past year had been worth it because now all would be calm and stable in our home. I assumed our biggest struggles were behind us, forgetting that, as Shakespeare tells us, "security is mortal's chief enemy."

That was the last time my daughter enjoyed unlimited innocence and happiness. When she and her two best friends arrived at the house, all three ran up the walk, charged into the front hall, and bounded up the stairs to her room.

"Come on, guys, it's down here on the left. Wait till you see it!" All three giggled and squealed. Jenna's face shone with anticipation and pride as she bubbled out what she loved about the new house and all her plans for it. Her friends agreed.

"Jenna, this upstairs deck is so cool." "Wow, I love the view from your room. You can see the fountain on the golf course." "And look, you have all this space. You've got the best room!"

"I know! Isn't it totally awesome?"

I just stood in the hall and listened, soaking in this moment of maternal fulfillment, so sure that I had done well by my children to see them so pleased.

Jenna caught the look on my face and skipped over to me.

"Mom, I am so, so happy. I love this house so much and we are going to be so happy here."

"I know, baby. I know we are."

Looking back, I suspect the demon was standing in the corner, smirking.

Chapter Two

One Hundred, Ten Pounds

I was grateful that we moved in on the first day of summer vacation, as our first few weeks in the house were busy with unpacking, establishing new routines and endless repair appointments from the builder. Until our refrigerator was delivered, we stored cold food day-to-day in an ice chest. Our meals were scattered and spontaneous. Each of us tried to find our own way of connecting with our new environment, both in private and shared spaces. Yet, a deadly negative energy had already occupied a place in Jenna's mind, and she seemed reluctant to even unpack her personal stuff.

Jenna's Journal

May 25

I feel so great. I'm so happy right now. Today marks our first week in the house. I have to say I love it here.

It's so strange, I think, that I am happiest when I am by myself. Is that abnormal for a seventeen year old not to enjoy talking or spending time with her friends? I honestly would just rather spend the summer by myself—reading, writing, listening to music, or being with my family—

> than to have to spend time with them. I don't understand why they want to do things with me... I am such a depressing, non-personality freak.
>
> That's another thing, what the hell has happened to me? Exactly when did I lose my spark? Whenever I am around people my own age, I act like an air-headed, shallow, uninteresting person. It's not like I am actually like that... but for some reason this altered personality takes over my body when I am around people and refuses to allow me to think for myself or say anything uncontrived. So I end up hating myself and envying those who aren't so cursed.

Because Tom and I were teachers, and consequently home all summer, we were around to notice the change in Jenna's behavior right away. It was little things at first. She would come down to the kitchen table every morning like always, sit and read the paper like always, but I would notice that after an hour sitting, she would leave the kitchen having not eaten. Then after each meal she started complaining of feeling nauseous, saying that eating made her sick. It didn't matter what the food was; she couldn't handle it. While before she would readily join me in grocery shopping, and actually seemed to enjoy sharing in this domestic task, now she kept finding excuses not to come along. She no longer wanted to join her stepdad and me on the deck at night for a Frappucino, didn't have the same interest in making salads together or having a friend over for dinner.

This slim, healthy girl also became obsessed with so-called fitness, and she began to jog on those hot summer mornings in the Phoenix valley to "get in shape." Never one to jog before, she now rose early to head out running. By seven a.m. in our urban desert, the sun is already pushing out ninety-plus degrees and promising rapidly increasing temperatures within hours. The air begins its impending stifle and all life takes on a slowed pace as heat radiates off sidewalk concrete. In this environment, one is *returning* from a jog by this early hour, if she knows what's good for her, not just starting out.

"Jenna, why have you decided to take up running, especially in this awful heat?"

"I'm not trying to lose weight or anything; I just want to get really fit. It feels good."

Off she ran.

An inkling. That's all it was at first. But one that gnawed away at me as I struggled to wrap my mind around this floating, uneasy sensation. Unwrap boxes, arrange drawers, fill out change-of-address cards, find a grocery store, meet the neighbors. But something is wrong.

Jenna's Journal

June 1

> I feel very fortunate. During the last month I went through such a decline; it really scared me. I was so incredibly stressed out because of the SATs and finals, plus moving, and I stopped eating… it's strange. I know I have a mentality very, very close to that of an anorexic. The only thing that stops me is the fact that I recognize it. So anyway, I wouldn't eat hardly anything, I was getting sick of my friends and boys, I was sick with stress and I cried myself to sleep every night. I was an

> incredible mess...but what scared me most was how well I hid it. Every night I would pray for God to get me out of it. And He did just in time. Everything ended just in time. We moved, the year ended, and I no longer had to spend so much mental energy worrying. I am so unbelievably grateful because I know that if I had gone much longer like that... well, nothing good would have happened. We'll say that.

This was the summer before Jenna's senior year in high school, and that meant it was time for her senior portrait. She and I shopped for a variety of outfits for her sitting. Her already slim form had now taken on new thinness, with hip bones protruding through thin shorts, and her collarbone poking out from her frame. Still, she looked lovely, downright womanly in the outfits she chose: a teal lace two-piece dress and a soft plum sweater with khaki slacks set. I still glance at these portraits today, musing how quickly and drastically her life was about to change and her appearance severely altered.

Jenna was taking a summer school class in the mornings, but was depressingly bored the rest of the day, spending hours at a time in her room. Every couple of days she made feeble attempts to find a job. Summers can be mercilessly long and still in the arid desert of Arizona. When afternoon temperatures reach one hundred and thirteen degrees, it becomes easy to adapt like the nearby lizards and just sit very still, waiting to be able to breathe lightly again with the fresher air of sundown. So at first I gave her space and asked little of her. But I was also fearful that long, empty afternoons can easily turn into deadly depressive weeks.

They did.

I offered the usual annoying "mom" clichés on ways to keep busy.

"Honey, why not call a friend and see a movie? How about checking out the new mall nearby? You know what would be fun? Try something new like ice-skating or something old like bowling. How 'bout it?"

"Mom, I just don't feel like it."

I kept expecting her to join in my enthusiasm to decorate our new home. We had spent nine months in those cracker-box apartments, while it was being built, planning, scheming, envisioning together how we would make this place ours. We pored over decorating magazines, watched endless makeover shows, and browsed through furniture stores for ideas. But now, I could not entice her to even emerge from her room. I told myself that she was just bonding with her new "digs" and soon she will come out with lots of plans for her own space. But she took no interest whatsoever, wouldn't put a thing on her walls, and did not care about linens or furnishings. The room remained bare and comfortless, with no sign of any personality inhabiting it. Jenna's sense of self seemed to recede into the pores of the walls to disappear.

"Honey, why don't you call Marie? I'm sure she's just as bored as you are."

"Sure, O.K."

But on she remained in her room for hours and days.

The demon had moved in, taking up space and energy. Jenna had found a companion.

Jenna's Journal

June 22

I am so sick of not having enough money and I'm sick of having to look longingly and disappointedly at material things and I'm sick of not wanting to talk to my own damn friends, and I'm sick of dreading a weekend at my father's and I'm sick of being hungry and I'm sick of hating me! And I'm sick of having every emotion known to man inside me but not being able to even talk about it, let alone write about it, and I'm sick of trying to plan my fucking future when I know it's doomed anyway, and I'm sick of turning out lights to save energy and I'm sick of worrying about finding true love when I know in my heart that I will never ever find it anyway and I'm sick of dumb boys because they're all the same when talking to me, and I'm so fucking sick of not ever being the girl, never the dream, never the inspiration. I'm going to go throw up now. Life is turning my stomach.

I felt innate mother-fears deep down in my bones, so deep I couldn't begin to give word form to them. Something very wrong was here among us, I knew. I tried to maintain a normal atmosphere in the house, tackling the all-consuming job of settling our family into our environment. But before anyone else in the family was aware, I began to notice signs of deceit in Jenna's eating and not eating. She had always "just eaten" or would "later." At dinner she took less and less food on her plate and tried to hide most under a napkin. *Do you think I don't notice? Do you think I don't see?* She would eagerly volunteer to clear the dinner table, scraping clean the plates of evidence, evidence of our eating and her not. Leftover food was put away with uncharacteristic haste.

One terrifying moment of truth came on a hot July morning as she came in from jogging, quickly scurried upstairs, and disappeared behind her bedroom door.

"Jenna, have you eaten any breakfast yet? You can't be out running in this heat without food," I called to her.

She murmured through her closed door, assuring me she had already eaten a muffin. For some reason, I felt a sting of doubt, compelled to take any measure to find out if she was telling the truth. I walked downstairs into the kitchen and found a half muffin on the counter. O.K., so she only had half. For a moment that hung suspended, I stood at the counter, numb, sensing that our entire relationship was about to shift. I slowly slipped my hand into the garbage disposal to feel the mushy crumbs of the other muffin half.

This was the defining moment, that second in time that draws a frozen line in the mind between then and now. This was the beginning of mistrust. I had thus far been blessed with a profoundly close relationship with my only daughter, I thought. Suddenly, we looked like every cliché of the adversarial parent-teenager scene. Trust is the delicate spider's thread binding people together. Powerfully strong when intact, shattering when broken.

I stood at that kitchen counter for what felt like years. My head spun as I tried to decode the moment. *O.K. What is happening here?* Everything I knew I no longer knew. Everything I believed as constant was in a sudden state of flux. In that tiny instant of seeming triviality, I felt the magnitude of dis-order.

Why is she lying to me? Why would she lie about eating?

I said nothing, but my mind's racing thoughts and fears spilled over themselves that day and days to come as I struggled to sort out the puzzle before me.

As my husband and I noticed her losing weight rapidly, we became increasingly alarmed. *What do we have on our hands?* I stifled my own sense of reason, insulated by the defense which denial provides. I could not utter the word, not even in my most private thoughts. But soon Tom and I both knew this had to be confronted.

"Jenna," I told her one afternoon, "we're concerned about you not being able to eat much lately. We want to make sure you are not losing too much weight. I want to weigh you."

"That's silly. I'm fine. Besides, it wouldn't be such a bad thing for me to lose a little weight. This is silly. You don't have to worry about me."

"Yes, well, I still want to check your weight. What were you before we moved into the house?"

"I don't know, I guess a hundred and twenty-five or thirty. Who cares? Weight doesn't matter."

"It does when it's an indication of illness. And all your talk about food making you feel sick lately really concerns me."

"Whatever."

So we weighed her. She had lost nineteen pounds in about a month, and was down to one hundred and ten pounds. Of course, she tried to reason our fears away.

"Mom, nothing's wrong. I'm just getting more fit. Don't worry about anything. I'm telling you, there's nothing wrong. Can I help you make dinner?"

Help me she would, seeming to have no discomfort around food preparation. In fact, she went out of her way to involve herself in the fixing of meals. I watched as she peeled, cut, sautéed, baked and served. Yet, she ate less and less once it was put in front of her. She became obsessed about a clean kitchen, constantly cleaning, wiping, putting food away, doing dishes, emptying the garbage. In moments of dark humor, I thought, well, at least there's one benefit to living in such an abnormal situation; my kitchen finally stays clean.

Jenna's Journal

July 5

Yesterday I got up late because I didn't have to run, and we took Tom out for a birthday breakfast. I had three freaking pancakes and orange juice and coffee. So I swore that I wouldn't eat anything for the rest of the day, which was okay, because even by 6:30 at Grandma's house I was still full and still energetic. But of course Grandma Jackie came up to me and gave me a five-minute lecture about how important the food pyramid is and that I needed protein from fatty hamburgers to burn up the fat from the carbs from the pancakes. So I ate a fucking hamburger to get her off my back, but you know, when I start eating I can't stop. So I ended the night hating myself for eating so much. It continues.

July 8

I can't win.

July 9

Where did all my zeal for life go??? I used to enjoy every day. Now I just wait for it to pass. I used to love writing and food and living, and now I don't even want to write in my journal anymore and every time I eat anything I feel like I can feel my hips and stomach getting fatter and my chin growing yet another layer. I feel weak but fat and I can't do anything about it at all!

I feel like I have nothing to offer this world. I am stupid, ugly, fat, with no self-esteem and no sense of humor.

All I want is to love life again. But how????

July 13

I can't take this anymore
My body is burning
melting
into the floor
I can't even stay up long enough
to pace
My mind drifts aimlessly
My body keeps gathering
and building
Beyond my own control.
There is literally *NOWHERE TO GO!*
No sights for my eyes to see
No enjoyment or love for my heart
to feast upon.
Seconds, minutes, hours pass like forevers.
I can't move.
And the more I think about it,

the less it all matters.
Hope for now,
for later
Keeps slipping away!
I can't think.
My idleness is killing me
and I can't do anything about it…
My heart
My head
My stomach
All empty.
One by choice.
I don't deserve.

By the end of July, Jenna was openly rejecting food, saying she always felt sick from eating. Yet soon she even complained of nausea before she had eaten, so food couldn't be to blame. What struck me as odd was that she didn't seem to be very disturbed by the fact that eating anything made her sick, so she said. She acted quite nonchalant about it all. So, food now makes me sick and I cannot eat at all… oh well. I didn't get it.

Jenna's Journal

July 14

At dinner Mom kept insisting that I eat more. Doesn't she know that the more people tell me to eat and try to force food down my throat, the less I want to eat?? And later I exercised, but I feel like it's no use—like I am going to be a fatty forever, and especially if Mom takes me to the doctor like she wants to—then I'll be forced to eat all the fucking time, and just the thought of that makes me not want to eat anything ever again. Can't people just leave me alone for once? Let me make my own decisions!

JULY 23

This morning I had an interview with a computer for Walgreen's and when I came home Mom and I had a painful, tearful talk. But despite the fact that I don't want to hurt my mom, I also hate the thought of food and its effect on me. So to cater to the two (pardon the pun), I think the only thing I can do is lie, which is wrong too, but I can't see any other way to make the both of us happy. I love her too much to keep ruining her life and happiness, and yet the very image of food makes me sick to my stomach.

JULY 29

Today I started my first job as a cashier at Walgreen's! Everyone was so-o-o nice. But I haven't eaten anything for a couple of days except for my Diet Dr. Pepper tonight, so I think the hunger plus the phenylalanine in my soda are working horrid wonders on my stomach. But I am sitting here writing in my journal and listening to jazz music and loving it, so I can't care. Besides, my thighs and legs and hips and stomach and waist and every one of my chins is still fat, so if I can still survive without food, why not go for it? It makes me feel better inside.

Tom and I insisted on weighing Jenna again. One hundred pounds. Twenty-nine pounds of my daughter were gone. And the ground beneath my feet turned to mush.

Chapter Three

One Hundred Pounds

Within these first weeks of hell, I knew in my gut what was happening, and I knew its possible consequences. By now, anyone would have labeled this an eating disorder, or *e.d.* in the current vernacular, and as a high school English teacher, I had seen cases over the years of its devastating effects. Senior girls wrote personal essays and research papers on the subject. Some confided in me as I tried to find the right help for them. Now I was looking at it sitting across from my kitchen table, yet it was hard to accept, particularly since Jenna didn't fit the so-called profile. I knew what had invaded the peace and well-being of our beautiful home and family. The demon had a name: Anorexia Nervosa.

Jenna's Journal

July 31

Have you ever felt like you are just completely drowning in a bottomless ocean of self-hatred? I feel like that often...especially in the last few months. I don't understand why or how long it will last, but I hope that someday soon someone will throw me a life preserver and draw me in so they can rub the salt from my eyes.

During that summer, I lay awake for hours each night, sifting through the day's details in order to decode this cryptic maze through which we were moving, grateful to not have classes to teach the next day. *I'm smart; I can figure this out.*

Many mornings I awoke at four a.m. with an anxious start of unknown origin. Then, in an instant, I was yanked back to the cause. *Oh, yes, I remember. Something malevolent is happening within these walls.* I would throw on my light cotton summer robe, unable to lie still with my thoughts crashing in a tidal wave, and walk through silent halls that still smelled of fresh paint and virgin carpet. These mornings were my private time while my family and my neighborhood slept on. I knew that once the day began I would have to be strong, wise, and in control. Mother. But daybreak was still all mine to share with the mourning doves that wouldn't tell on me. My feet often found their way back upstairs and out to the deck where I stripped all veneer and sobbed uncontrollably, burying my face in a kitchen towel to stifle my guttural groans.

Cool desert breezes belied the day's oncoming unrelenting heat. In silent communion with the magentas and golds of the sun's rise in the desert's eastern horizon, my aloneness felt both more blessed, while more frightening. Nature seemed paradoxically indifferent and reassuring at the same time. I mentally yelled and screamed and lashed out at the heavens, soaking my towel with tears of terror. *Why my daughter? Why to such a bright, stable, loved girl? Why now, when everything was falling into place in our lives? Oh my God, why?*

The quiet of those solitary dawns drew me toward old prayers of the catechism of my youth. I talk to my God intimately; prayer for me has always been more of a conversation than the formulaic memorized lyrics of my childhood religious training in Catholicism. I was surprised to find myself conjuring old, musty verses long buried. No longer dismissing them as meaningless words delivered in robotic rote, I needed their centuries-old structure to control my thoughts when my mind and heart had no form, and I quietly uttered each word with new-found sincerity and understanding. I rediscovered the rhythm, the poetry, the very music of traditional prayer, finding comfort in the familiar.

When I was a child, snooping in my mother's bedside table, I found a tiny prayer book that captured my attention. Only about five inches square, its cover, hard-molded in a laminated casing yellowed with time, had little metal hinges, allowing one to snap the miniature missal closed like a box. Wow, I thought, a book that locks, in a way. One of the gilded-edged pages held a prayer which I was never taught in catechism, not part of the rosary, never heard in Mass.

No one made me learn this one prayer, but I did. I was enchanted, lured in by the magic of the words. Looking back, perhaps this prayer was embedded in my brain and soul in order to serve me so many years later when I would need it. Perhaps our everyday moments are laid out for us as preparation and we don't even know it, as a sort of Divine choreography.

Now, in my time of need, how natural it all felt to sense this prayer rising to my consciousness: I turned to Mary. Naturally. Our ultimate Mother will understand my pain and fear and intercede on my behalf. Truly, she must hear me in my time of direst need. I relied on her advocacy in Heaven. She will know.

And out seeped the prayer of my youth, *Salve Regina*:

> Hail holy Queen, Mother of Mercy,
> our life, our sweetness, and our hope.
> To thee do we cry, poor banished children of Eve.

> To thee do we send up our sighs, mourning and weeping
> in this valley of tears.
> Turn then, most gracious advocate,
> thine eyes of mercy toward us,
> and after this, our exile,
> show unto us the blessed fruit of thy womb, Jesus.
> Oh clement, oh loving, oh sweet Virgin Mary,
> pray for us, oh Holy Mother of God,
> that we may become
> worthy of the promises of Christ.

I am sure the words themselves bewildered the little girl who found them: *advocate, exile, clement. Huh?* After all, what can a child know of the travails of life? How little I understood as a child; how much I would understand later. Somehow, the very music of this lyrical language conveyed its sorrowful, yet comforting, tone. Perhaps we need to imprint our children at tender ages with the phraseology that will serve them later in life, for now this prayer had come back to me as a belated gift. I felt overcome with deep devotion to Mary, the Mother of all mothers, who knows the pain of losing her child and surely hears my fearful plea. *Mary, whose goddess power my church alone honors, hear my prayer. Help this humble mother.*

Mother. The very word is synonymous with nurture. I now felt myself failing in this essential role. No amount of reasoning, pleading or coercing made a dent in my daugher's rejection of food. One day, in a moment of desperation, I sat my Jenna down on the sofa and, taking her hand in mine, tried to explain to her the impact all of this was having on me.

"My dear daughter, I am your mother. Since you were born it has been my fundamental job to nourish and nurture you. And now you are not letting me do *my job*," as I choked on tears. She responded with a far-away look of incomprehension.

Never have I faced such a defiant roadblock to my primary mission in life. A single mom for eight years, I often felt like the circus act of keeping plates spinning as I struggled to maintain the balance of pursuing a master's degree, teaching full-time, trying to re-establish a social life, all the while rearing happy, healthy children, and I had done a damn good job. Now, I was thrown back to the fundamentals of feeding my child, the defiant two-year-old with her mouth closed. I felt powerless. And very afraid.

Paramount in my life was the security of my three children's mental and emotional health. I grew up with a father who suffered a lifetime of emotional illness, and I knew its devastating toll on my mother, sister, and me. I vowed this would not happen in my own family. Protect the spirit. Foster the self-esteem. Nourish the soul. These were my edicts and I worked hard to maintain them. I thought I had read all the right parenting books, watched all the proper expert talk shows, and was beginning to reap the rewards of this noble, sacrificial mission I pridefully trumpeted. That dangerous complacency again. My children had so far avoided the societal traps of drugs, alcohol and other extreme behaviors. We laughed a lot in our family, talked about everything, and readily said "I love you." No, we were not the illusive perfect family, but I knew my children were becoming equipped to handle life. At least I thought so.

But we are never truly out of the woods, are we? If others tend to blame parents when the sons or daughters falter or lose their way, believe me, we parents do, too. I now questioned everything about my parenting and came away with no answers. No hint of a reason for this nightmare my daughter was living. But it must be my fault. It must have been something I did or didn't do, said or didn't say. You worry for your child that a disease, an accident or the bogey man might get him or her. You do not lie awake at night with fears that your child's enemy is herself turning inward toward self-destruction. What kind of insanity is that?

I needed to let others in our family know what was going on with Jenna. I called her father.

"Yeah, I kind of noticed that, myself," Jim told me. "When we spent those couple of days in San Diego, Jenna wasn't eating much around us. I just figured she was on a diet or going through a girl thing. I didn't think much about it, actually," he explained.

"Well, I'm getting very, very worried. When you spend time with her, please make yourself aware of her eating habits. I just have an awful feeling about this, Jim."

"O.K., Valerie. Will do."

The most difficult call went to my mother. With my voice trembling, almost in a whisper, I said, "Mom, Jenna isn't eating."

"What do you mean she isn't eating?"

Try explaining a mental illness to someone when you don't understand it yourself. It never goes smoothly.

My girl was not eating. *No, I don't know why. Yes, I told her that. Yes, she knows that. No, I haven't. Yes, I did. No, I don't think so. Yes, I am sure. No, I can't. Yes, I am taking action.* This became a frequent refrain of mine.

A most baffling disease, this anorexia nervosa. In a sense, one is addicted to a non-behavior, to not eating. This conundrum struck at the very core of my dear mother. A Depression baby, World War II bride, and devoted student of *Good Housekeeping* standards for homemaking, my mother was a great cook who crawled into bed at night with her favorite reading material—a cookbook—and she saw food as a central point of discourse and cure for all that ails ye. *Stomachache? You're hungry. Feeling tired? You haven't eaten enough lately. Caught a cold? It's because you haven't been eating well. Clean your plate. Two vegetables and dessert with every meal. Mom, we just got back from vacation. How was the food? How are you, Mom? Oh, fine, we're having spareribs tonight.* Now, with all of these messages playing in our heads, my sister, Marsha, and I should be grossly overweight, right?

Yet, no one in my family was ever too heavy or too thin. However, we also grew up in a culture where most females' conversations were punctuated with words like *thin*, *diet*, and *do I look fat in this*? My sister and I were never fat, and even as I write this it comes as a revelation, because I think we always thought we were. Like most adolescent girls, we always wished we were thinner. Marsha was the disciplined dieter who'd begin each summer inspired to try the latest wacky diet: boiled eggs and chicken breasts, grapefruit, miracle soup, nothing but hot dogs for a week. But I was not that disciplined. I would cut back or cut out. My petite mom would go through her mental self-flagellation from time to time and lose an easy five pounds, adamant about never going over what she decided was her ideal number on the scale. A stunning woman into her eighties, she continued to be concerned about gaining weight. So my own relationship with food was paradoxical; it is the all-consuming panacea… but you'd better not get fat.

As an adult, my body image was skewed. I still saw myself as heavy. I'm sure I made the typical comments around my own children about wanting to lose weight, especially as it fluctuated with each childbirth. But while raising my children, I tried to minimize food issues around the house. I didn't want it to be such a big focus, either as an enemy or a friend. I had goodies around the house, but not an abundance of them. We enjoyed cookies or ice cream, but didn't "pig out."

The mind of an anorexic's mom wanders through knotted mental labyrinths, searching for clues and keys. I pounded my way through memories and emotional tapes. *Just tell me why it happened, and if you can't, at least tell me how to fix it.* I was prepared to lay blame on myself, because a devastating answer is better than none at all. Despite my inability to wrap my thoughts around any concrete reason for Jenna's illness, I still concluded it must have been me somehow.

Many nights, long after everyone went to bed, I sat for hours, re-visiting happier times, huge family photo albums stacked all around me. I ran my fingers over hundreds of photos, smiling softly at images of my pregnant days, babies taking their first baths in the kitchen sink, birthday cake smeared on two-toothed grins. Baby Jenna's brown-eyed, moonfaced glow sprinkled over page after page of family photographs, and I was still struck by how stunningly beautiful a child she was.

With that beauty came a strong, independent will that gave me many a challenge. When Jenna was four, she suffered from asthma and, following hospitalization, was prescribed a daily medication in the form of a capsule. Each day when we got home from school, I would mix her capsule with a spoon of her favorite strawberry ice cream. Usually, not a problem. But one day, for whatever reason, she simply announced she would not take the pill. Forty-five minutes later, she swallowed. For *forty-five minutes* we stood in the kitchen in composed battle. Daughter determined. Mother resolute. Even once the spoonful was in her mouth, there she still stood, refusing to swallow. Forty-five minutes is a long time to stand in a kitchen at the end of a long day. But stand we both did. I knew that, as the mom, if I lose this battle to a four-year-old, I have surely lost the war.

I won the battle that day. But I was also served a dose of the extremities of my daughter's fierce obstinance. And now, thirteen years later, I was filled with fear that should she win this battle, I will lose her. *Once again, I cannot let you win, daughter. Once again, I am fighting for your health, for your very life. I will not lose. I cannot!*

Jenna's Journal

August 5

Lately I am always either bingeing or starving. I can't find a happy medium in anything anymore, including self-confidence or eating habits or emotions. I am so incredibly angry at so many people that I can't stand it—or them—any more.

August 10

This fear, this loneliness, this deception
of the mind
is a wall being built up
slowly, carefully,
stone by fiery stone
inside me
and around me
closing in, until I must
crash through.
But it pains me so, because
I know that it's
my hand
laying the bricks.

Within the first few weeks I had called our local clinic to have my daughter seen by a doctor. I was told they could not get us in for three more agonizing weeks. I tried to assure myself that we could wait, but through those weeks we watched Jenna's behaviors intensify and her emotional and mental connection to the world around her begin to fray.

Right before school started, Jenna was finally examined by a young doctor, so young, in fact, that it was her first day on the job at this clinic, perhaps as a doctor at all. I began our visit by showing the doctor Jenna's senior portrait, Jenna now looking nothing like that, and informing her, "This is my daughter, Jenna. You don't know her, but she isn't like the girl in this room. Please help us."

I knew that anyone could see the glaring contrast. Jenna's full face was now hollowed out and gaunt. Her coloring had changed from rosy to a sort of pale yellowish-green, the posture of a lively young woman now drawn down like one who is tired and old. *Can't you see? Can you not see?* I wanted to scream, seeing the doctor's passive expression.

Jenna acted flippant about the whole thing, pretending this was an attempt to address some digestive problem that was making eating distressful for her. Questions were superficially asked and superficially answered. Weight recorded: ninety pounds. Temperature and blood pressure taken. Perfunctory examination performed. The physician seemed particularly uncomfortable and unprepared to deal with what we all knew by now was an eating disorder. Like the proverbial elephant in the room, the demon was right there beside us, and no one wanted to address him by name.

I wanted the doctor to say the words. I needed her to validate the truth.

"Well, yes, Jenna," she said in a tepid tone, "you need to eat, honey. Maybe you have a nervous stomach."

Antacids prescribed. Counseling recommended. Off you go.

Chapter Four

Ninety Pounds

As summer ended and I faced the inevitable return to my teaching job, and Jenna's return to school, I worried that without my presence around her throughout the day, her behavior and health would deteriorate. She was carrying a full schedule: Math, English, Psychology, Physics, Drama, Government. Jenna always loved school, and had always talked about how her senior year would be the best. Instead, she began this final year in high school looking completely unfamiliar to her friends. Having kept herself isolated from them all summer, they were not prepared for what they saw. By now, having lost thirty-nine pounds in a couple of months, she took on a distorted look. Her new school clothes hung disinterested on her bony form. Her cheeks sunk in and her knees knocked together in grotesque knobbiness. Her hair was now dry and flyaway, somehow looking thicker in relation to her shrinking frame. She looked unrecognizable from that senior portrait.

Yet each friend was afraid to say anything. Language takes thought or feeling from the abstract to the concrete, adding form to its function. It makes the unthinkable real. If we don't give something a label, if we let it float in our brains like mere wisps of energy, it remains intangible and we remain free. But to speak the word seems to construct a sort of plastic mold around the shapeless, and then we have to claim it and deal with it. It is there. So in a subtle form of self-defense, while Jenna's friends were shocked upon seeing her when school started, they said nothing for several weeks. Silence is denial.

Back-To-School applied to everyone in our family. Nathan was now a junior at Arizona State University, Jenna and Greg in high school, Tom was teaching at our nearby community college, and I taught high school English. Suddenly, everyone got very busy. I couldn't know what Jenna ate for breakfast or lunch. All I knew were two things: she was not eating with us at home, and she was clearly losing more weight. Worst of all, her spirit was changing. Throughout these first few months, my daughter had turned from a viewpoint of lightness and peace to the opaque vapors of depression. She became belligerent whenever we confronted her on the eating issue. She distanced herself from her brothers, showing little or no interest in their lives, and kept more and more to herself, alone in a mental box with her demon.

Jenna's Journal

August 18

> Today was the second day of school and things seemed to be going accordingly. I like my classes and my friends. I feel like I'm living two separate lives: one at school with my friends, and one at home. It's strange.

As the new school year started, I let my friends know, one at a time, what was happening so that if I started sobbing in my beer at happy hour for no apparent reason, they'd understand. I managed to lead an all-day faculty workshop, hanging on to my focus without a single blip, but as soon as it ended, I walked over to Joanne, a longtime colleague, and whispered, "Jenna isn't eating." I didn't know how else to approach the subject. Is there another way to say it? She looked back at me as if to say, *When did you start speaking Japanese?* Next, I sat down in the office of my close friend, Donna, a school counselor, and poured it all out. She listened intently, with her characteristic loving concern.

Finally, she leaned in close to my face and spoke softly. "Val, honey, you'd better prepare yourself. It's very likely Jenna will need hospitalization. That's the usual course."

The thought gripped me with new anxiety. *Really?* I thought. *My daughter? Surely a few counseling sessions and she'll snap out of this.*

"Oh, not that," I said. "No, Jenna will come out of this O.K. She just needs some good therapy."

"O.K., hon, but if they recommend hospitalization, you have to trust them. They know what they're doing."

"I am so scared, Donna. I can't put it into words. This is so hard."

"I know, sweetie. I know."

"No. You do not," I said, with a quiet firmness. I was surprised to hear myself saying even that much. The nasty energy I was now living around sat on my shoulder making me want to scream, *You don't have children of your own. You cannot, can not even begin to know. Don't insult me by claiming off-handedly that you know. You love me and you love Jenna. But you cannot know the place in which I am standing. This is for the mother alone.* But I am glad I didn't say more at that moment. Donna knew from a counselor's vantage, she knew as a friend. She was all she could be for me. But she could not truly know.

That night, when Jenna was again unable to force herself to join us for dinner, Tom took my hands in his and spoke in the cautious tone of a new stepparent. "Valerie, we've got to move to the next step. We're getting nowhere with this."

"Oh, I know, I know. What do we do?"

The next day I called our health plan and was assigned a psychiatrist in their directory to call for an appointment. We had Jenna evaluated by him the following week. Having already learned much about the complexities of this disorder and its multitudes of causes and ramifications, we found it appalling that after only one thirty-minute interview with Jenna, this professional got out his broad brush and with a stroke concluded that she was not anorexic because she didn't think herself to be fat. *Oh, really?* This points to one mask the demon wears that strengthens it. Health professionals still struggle to fully understand this disorder. "It's about weight and dieting." "It's about control." "It's about a dysfunctional family structure." "It's about coming out of abuse." "It's about a culture that celebrates thinness." "It's about insecurity." "It's about...." Jenna didn't fit these pathologies. Or did she? Did I know my daughter at all? Could I really say what was in her mind and heart, despite what I thought was a tight bond between us? Only long after this did I see the clues that many, if not all, adolescent girls try to keep secret. This is a time of overwhelming, stifling insecurity, when the self-image, distorted as it usually is for us all, becomes the reality. My daughter always seemed secure in her self-esteem, but was she really? What, then, was going on? Which was the truth—her apparent mental health, or her obvious mental illness? What secrets lie? And where do we go from here?

By now, Jenna exhibited severe bruising all over her legs due to malnutrition, and Tom and I became so desperate over her state one Sunday afternoon that we took her to the emergency room. After waiting for three hours, we were told with apologetic smiles that there was nothing they could do. Nothing? Nothing. We felt powerless.

Back we returned to the family physician. More tests revealed that she was dehydrated. In the hospital for rehydration. Out again for more starvation.

Eventually, I called another psychologist and begged for action. "There must be something, something we can do for her!" I shrieked into the phone. "I have sat here on hold for thirty-four minutes waiting to talk to you. I am a desperate mother. My daughter is dying! Please, please help us. Tell me what the hell I am supposed to be doing, because I am lost!"

He referred us to one of the leading residential hospitals for eating disorders in our area—Willow Creek. While their actual clinic was several miles outside the greater Phoenix area, they maintained a satellite residential wing in Scottsdale, thirty minutes from our home in suburban Gilbert and just five minutes from where my parents lived. I wouldn't put this off for one more day. On my insistence, they scheduled Jenna to be evaluated at Willow Creek the next evening. As soon as she came home from school, I explained what she and I would be doing in a few hours. She gave me an icy stare and barked, "Whatever." I called my sister who also lived near the hospital and told her, "Marsha, I am so nervous. Tom has night class and I can't do this alone."

"Don't say another word," she said. "I'll meet you there. Everything will be fine, Valerie."

"Thank you so much." I was quickly learning how to ask for help, something which, up until then had always been difficult for me.

Jenna and I sat in the sterile lobby, she with shoulders hunched over, me with hands folded white-knuckled tight, neither one speaking. Frankly, I wasn't there to please her; I didn't care what she thought of me or of this entire scheme. I was grateful to see my sister walk through the sliding door with hugs for us. She tried in vain to make syrupy small talk with us both. Didn't work. Neither of us could fake niceties that night. I was stone-frightened; Jenna was shut down. *Sorry, Marsha. Normal just can't survive in some settings.*

Finally, I was called in to answer a few preliminary questions as the parent of the minor. Then Jenna had her interview in private. Marsha and I sat in silence for what seemed like hours, but was actually about thirty minutes. The director of the facility told me in private that Jenna warranted further evaluation and directed us to bring her in for a two-day observation. I signed some papers, hugged my sister, and home we went. Jenna seemed completely drained from the evening and didn't ask me any questions, so I put off telling her of Willow Creek's request until the next morning. When I did, I couldn't believe how passively she went along with the plan. By this time, Jenna was so detached from the present moment; her brown eyes looked back at me in a vacant look of detachment. But when we explained that this action meant admitting her into this hospital for a couple of days, she pleaded with us to give her a chance to show that she could whip this on her own.

"Please, please, Mom, let me show you I can do it. I can. I will. I promise. Just give me more of a chance to prove it. Please!"

"O.K., sweetie." I didn't want to face any of this either, and I buckled. "But if you can't, we will be taking you to Willow Creek."

"Thank you, Mommy." She squeezed me tight.

Jenna's Journal

August 21

> So here's the bottom line: the doctors have diagnosed me with anorexia, although I am not sure I believe in it myself.

For the next day or two, she bounced into the house from school in an artificial zeal and announced how she had had actual cravings for Subway sandwiches, indulging in a turkey sub each day at lunch. I tried to believe this was great progress, but doubted its authenticity.

"That's terrific, sweetie. I'm glad you're eating and enjoying it."

"Oh, yeah, Mom. Really, they're delicious. I'm really doing fine now."

But beyond these daily outbursts of optimism at four p.m. every afternoon, nothing changed. She still never ate around us, still remained very depressed, and even after a couple of days, the Subway sandwich chapter was over as quickly as it came. I gave her that week to convince us, only to watch her withdraw more. She was crashing.

Worrying about her despondency, and suffering my own anxiety over the painful decision I was about to make, I whisked her off for an evening of mother-daughter quality time at the mall, removed from the suffocating atmosphere within our walls of our house, a house which now seemed to inhale and exhale some alien breath. We both went through the motions of a false air of normalcy, acting like it was just another shopping trip. But our small talk was stilted, our eyes avoided each other's.

While she roamed through a poster store, I slipped into a gift shop and bought a handful of little polished stones, each with a word pressed and painted in gold. Throughout that long week I would leave one on her pillow, or in other unexpected places, to remind her of the power that words can imprint on our spirits. The first was a magenta stone offering TRUST. WISDOM in amethyst followed, along with LOVE in rose quartz, PEACE in jasper, COURAGE in agate. Even at the time it seemed simplistic and cliché, but I felt so utterly helpless, wishing I could force such attributes into her skin. If these abstract ideas came jarred in honey form, I would have spread it over my daughter's body in hopes of coating her soul.

By the end of the week I had to confront her with the truth that she wasn't eating. In tears, she sighed in resignation and agreed, seeming almost relieved by the intervention. Tom and I sat down privately with her two brothers and tried to explain how their sister would be getting some help for a couple of days. We downplayed our own sense of urgency, but wanted them to be aware of the seriousness of the situation. Nathan and Greg both sat quietly, looking sad, holding in any questions they may have had.

"Just do whatever she needs, Mom. We love her and want her to be O.K. again," Nate finally said.

"Yeah, we miss the old Jenna," whispered Greg.

With each step our family took on this journey together, I felt the road forking and turning sharply at any moment, with no known destination.

On Sunday my daughter packed a few things, and Tom and I drove her to Willow Creek's satellite facility. None of us said a word as we drove the interminably long twenty-five minutes to the hospital. As freeway traffic sped past us, my mind drifted. *I wonder where all these people are going.*

Are they on their way to work on a Sunday? To visit friends? To spend birthday money at the mall? To the lake? To attend church? Where are all your normal lives taking you? Are YOU on your way to commit YOUR daughter to residential treatment?

Pulling into the parking lot, I tried in vain to coerce my stomach into lowering itself down out of my esophagus. Cold sweat rolled over me, and as Tom killed the engine I felt the obnoxious betrayal of tears try to make their appearance. *No, no, I cannot give in to emotions. I have got to get through this. I have got to get us all through this. I can cry later. Yes, I can cry much later. My job here is to be strong, in control, and self-assured. I am the adult, damn it. I am the mother.*

Tom carried Jenna's red and blue plaid duffel bag; she carried her oversized stuffed basset hound, Poppyseed. I carried my resolve. We each had to sign in at the front desk, then were led down one hall and out a back door. We walked along a diagonal courtyard and I noticed a small volleyball court and picnic tables everywhere. It was a gorgeous September afternoon, but no one was outside. Residents knew where they were, and it wasn't the Holiday Inn.

We entered another wing of the hospital, were seated in a small cubicle, and were given a thick stack of forms to fill out. *O.K., I can do that.* I was grateful for the focus of something to do. I gave a cursory read and signature to Conditions of Admission, Medical Treatment Agreement, Authorization Agreements, Patient Rights and Responsibilities, Grievance Procedure, Disclosure on Medication Use, Discrimination Policy, Important Drug Information As we floated numbly through paperwork, trying to maintain our dignity, I tried to absorb my child's new surroundings and noticed that the halls were lined with elderly people in wheelchairs or on gurneys, each one alone and looking completely spent of physical and mental health, their eyes saying they were ready to die. It was a devastating scene of despair. And it smelled funny. *Oh God, tell me I am not leaving my daughter in this setting.* It was soon explained to us that Willow Creek did not have its own residential wing at this facility; it was housed within the adult section of a larger behavioral hospital, but separated. So Jenna was assigned to the general adolescent psychiatric hall for teens with a multitude of serious mental problems. I didn't know this before; I assumed she would be strictly with other young people with the same problem. By now I felt so confused, almost held captive myself, not knowing what to expect next.

That was the source of our horror those first days—no one explained to us what to expect from all these procedures. This was their daily routine, but it was not ours. All we were prepared for was a two-day evaluation. We were told she would be observed, then a plan of action would be determined, when, in fact, they know this as the precursor to long-term hospitalization. We had no idea we had just relinquished control of our daughter's life to unfamiliar professionals. "It's only for two days, Jenna, just two days," we had told her, in very honest naiveté, thinking that stint would make her fine. How foolish.

A tall, young, athletic man with kind eyes led the three of us down another hall to Jenna's wing. Introducing himself as Ray, an intern, he spouted house rules to us while we walked. I was so relieved to leave the pre-death corridor of age and Alzheimer's. While Jenna was taken away to be weighed (later recorded at eighty-five pounds), her bag was checked for contraband; we had been briefed in advance of the long list of forbidden items that could conceivably be used in self-abuse or cheating. It read like prison:

NO radios
NO cd players
NO cell phones
NO cameras
NO musical instruments
NO clocks with cords
NO plastic bags
NO liquid bleach
NO food, gum or beverage from outside
NO aluminum cans
NO rat-tailed combs
NO pagers
NO electric toothbrushes
NO cowboy boots
NO hard-toed shoes
NO hats or caps
NO bandanas

Contraband items kept at nurse's station and returned immediately after use:

glass items
blow dryers
aerosol cans
perfume or cologne
curling irons
nail polish
laundry detergent

Contraband items locked in medication room:

razors
nail clippers
nail polish remover
medicated topicals

I understood well enough the intent of banning these materials; the young and suffering in this world will find ingenious ways to hurt themselves or others. But reading through the rules, I felt embarrassingly sheltered about life, and knew I had entered a whole new culture.

Jenna rejoined us and we now stood at double doors with windows. Locked. Ray took out a large ring of keys and with an air of one authorizing access to an armory, we entered the adolescent wing of Desert Samaritan Hospital.

A tiny space of about six feet by seven feet served as the entire "hangout" area for the teens to sit, read, watch t.v., play cards. There was nowhere near enough seating for the eight or so young adults in this cramped living room setting, so a natural pecking order clearly determined who had to sit on the floor. Every single time I walked through this area in the coming weeks, more times than I wanted to count, the television was on and tuned to the worst that broadcasting has to offer, usually *The Jerry Springer Show*. I was appalled that these troubled kids were allowed to fill their heads with such cultural crap depicting more scenarios of totally dysfunctional, fucked-up lives, perhaps even worse than theirs. Maybe that's why they liked to watch it. Or maybe they didn't give their viewing even a thought as they sat in stony silence gazing at the screen, more likely drifting off to their own points of pain. The whole scene made me sick.

Those not watching t.v. were usually engaged in agitated talk on this or that teen topic, although the ridiculously loud television prevented meaningful conversation. That day, and every other we came to visit, everyone would stop what they were doing and size us up with looks of mistrust. I tried to give them a mom/teacher smile, weak though it must have been.

Ray now took us into Jenna's room. Two twin beds, one plain nightstand between them, a desk, two small closets, one bathroom. Very stark, except for the brightly-colored chenille bedspreads and orange shag carpeting.

Until now, we three had barely made eye contact. So much to take in. I tried to put the cheery Mom spin on things in a ridiculous attempt to sound light and optimistic.

"This is very roomy. It's really pretty nice, honey. Oh, and look, Jenna, there is a beautiful huge tamarack tree outside your window. See, if you stand along the wall here and look out at just a certain angle you can see a bit of it. Gosh, it's so beautiful out today. Fall is definitely in the air. Maybe some of the other kids would like to play volleyball later. You always liked volleyball. I like these daisy bedspreads. I wonder if you have a roommate. Did you remember all of your toiletries?" I must have sounded like an imbecile. Like the Mom PLAY button got stuck.

Anyone who speaks *mother* knows we sometimes must speak in code. "Wear a sweater tonight." (*I love you.*) "Did you get enough to eat?" (*I love you.*) "Let's go buy you some new shoes for school." (*I love you.*) "Your violin solo in the fourth grade concert sounded great!" (*I love you.*) Standing in that room, all my silly verbal spinning could have been decoded as this: "I love you, I love you. I am so scared. I don't want to leave you. I want you to be okay. I want this new environment to be friendly and safe. I want you to find comfort. I hope you don't hate me. I hope we're doing the right thing. God Almighty, I hope this works."

Jenna now sat on the bed, clinging to Poppyseed, seeming in some fog of disbelief. Her stringy, matted hair hung long around her shoulders. By now she had taken to wearing only shapeless, dull-colored, ugly clothes and they draped her body like a thin heap of old, soiled rags. She just sat, looking far away.

I moved across the room to sit down next to her. Tom joined us, and the three of us remained completely motionless for what seemed more like hours than the minutes they were. There just didn't seem to be anything left to say. I held her soft hands in mine, and for once, Mom couldn't think of a single word to utter.

Finally, we reached the dreaded moment of leaving her. She and I stood in the doorway close enough to inhale each other's breath, both of us shaking in fear. Tom stood in respectful silence alongside. Time froze. Jenna's pained look to us spoke of terror and confusion and a hateful begging to not go, not leave her. My eyes betrayed my unspoken pleading for her forgiveness. As I took hold of her icy-cold bony hands, I slipped a last stone into her palm, clasped her fingers around it, praying to myself that she would some day understand what we were doing, and in the meantime not throw away the azure stone that read: *HOPE.*

It was the most difficult day of my life. My daughter was locked up.

Giving her one last mother's hug, and pulling myself away from her arms, I flashed back to Jenna at age five. Swimming lessons. I had to leave her at the public pool in the very capable hands of the swimming instructor, but my strong-willed daughter would make me pay. She tugged and pulled and fidgeted. Her screaming and pleading went on for so many minutes that I thought the instructor would ask me to withdraw her from the class. "Don't leave me! Don't go! Please, please, mommy, no. Take me from here! I don't want this! No-o-o!"

"But honey, you need this. You have to learn to swim. I know what I'm doing." Then the ultimate parental cliché, "It's for your own good."

More screaming. Cars blocks away braking sharply, drivers turning toward the desperate sounds of what surely had to be a young child being horribly abused. Oh—just another mother enforcing swimming lessons.

That day at the pool, I finally just walked away, still hearing her nerve-shattering cries behind me, but never turning around to look back. I must not. My legs got me to the car where I sat and waited out the forty-five minute lesson, knowing that I was being a good mom. It's what I had to do and it felt right. But the emotional strains were wrenching.

Years later when Jenna, as an incoming high school freshman, bluntly announced she'd be joining the high school's swim team, I just smiled to myself in sweet vindication.

Now I was turning to walk away again, this time her screams silent, but felt, and with the stakes much higher.

Chapter Five

Eighty-Five Pounds

In giving birth, we break the cardinal rule of gambling: *Never risk more than you are prepared to lose.* With each infant girl or boy we metaphorically lift high in the air as an offering to Life, we dare to wager that which is most dear and valuable to us—that which we are clearly not willing to lose to the game. We place our very offspring on this sort of Roulette wheel and as it spins, we pray, pray, pray, whisper silent or wailing loud, *Please spare my wager. Please do not allow me to lose. I cannot lose.* Terrible, sloppy, foolish gamblers, we parents. We wear a delicate skin of faith under which lurks fear. I was not, nor ever will be, prepared to lose any child of mine, especially to what I thought, at the time, was an obscenely "curable" disease. But the world of eating disorders is baffling and complex. And not so easily cured.

Walking away from Willow Creek that day, my silly feet plodded one in front of the other. Finally Tom and I found ourselves back at the car. *What happens now? What will they do to her? For her? Did we do the right thing? Oh God, did we?* We sat in the front seat for a very long time until Tom started the ignition. The abrasive sound grated on my heart.

Ironically, that night when my head sunk down onto my pillow, sleep came with more peace than I had known for months. Jenna was in someone else's care. She was being watched over by professionals. It was out of my pitifully amateur hands, for a time, and I slept in deep relief. And emotional exhaustion.

That night also marked my return to an old friend, the blank notebook, and as I had in years past, I found myself compelled to write as an outlet, a private companion, sometimes directed to Jenna, in recording what I sensed was a very important time. I opened my small spiral-bound, deep emerald, crushed-velvet-covered journal and wrote.

Mother's Journal Entry

It's one hour later. I am trying not to cry at your Grandma Mickey and Grandpa Tom's. Grandma keeps saying she prays for you every night. Grandpa holds my hand and in the childlike way as an Alzheimer's sufferer utters with effort, "I'm sorry." Two hours later Tom and I are at Vito's Italian restaurant. I'm drinking red wine for the first time in years. I'm relying on it to dull the pain. I'm afraid to be in public, but Tom probably reasons that will help hold me together. It does, but I still quietly cry unashamedly; I don't care. It's 5:00. We left you three hours ago. I miss you—I ache for you. I can't stop crying. Tom strokes my hair. Nate is home after 6:00. He is so worried and needs to be in on everything. 8:30—Dad and Greg come in. Your dad is so distraught over you—tearful. I wonder if he plans to visit you. 9:30—Nate, Greg, Tom and I are all in the living room. Nate's interviewing Tom and me about our visit to Ireland for his culture class at ASU. I miss you in this family scene. Where is

Jenna? Where is my healthy, happy daughter???
10:00 I fall asleep in a dull oblivion.

This morning at 4 a.m. I wake with a panicked start and blurt out your name, "JENNA!"

8:30 I call Grandma—"She doesn't want visitors, Mom, so I'll bring her the Teddy Bear you bought for her."

You've been gone one day. One day. Or has it been an eternity? What are they doing there to you and for you? What are you doing there for yourself? Are you eating? What? Are you hating us, missing us? Do you want to see us?

God, I miss you so much, Jenna-pie. You seeped into my thoughts at every second of my teaching day. Wonder if anyone noticed.

Daily life became difficult for our two boys. They understood even less than we. They felt even more powerless than we. They were afraid to ask questions, afraid to make me cry. Afraid to cry themselves. They weren't even sure of the questions to ask about this mysterious, predominantly female illness.

The air within our home became thick with tension. None of us really knew what was happening, but toxic fumes of fear and despair permeated the rooms. We were in the first year in this new house, one for which we had struggled and sacrificed so much. It represented our beginning family structure, now finally under one roof. But through these first months, as we chose window coverings and planned landscaping, we were juxtaposed with the disturbing, terrifying family crisis within that we could not ignore. This was indeed our best and worst of times. We were trying desperately to make all the rest of our lives normal, but it couldn't really be, could it? Jenna needed us now; the time would come later for having friends over and good times.

At the time of Jenna's admittance, Tom and I were given reams of materials to read to rapidly educate ourselves and family members on the subject of eating disorders. *A Glossary of Terms, "What Do We Do Now?" Family Involvement and Role of Siblings, Goal-setting, Helpful Supplemental Readings on Eating Disorders.* We read what to say and not say, do and not do in aiding our girl toward recovery. "Praise your child for accomplishments, not physical appearance; in fact, never mention it." "Don't obsess about your own extra five pounds or so, or call dessert a 'bad food.'" "Do not disparage overweight or underweight people."

But then, contradictions emerged. "Don't force your child into eating." Yet, "Make it clear to your child you will not let her starve." "Maintain a normal atmosphere about eating and dinners." Yet, "Do not insist your child participate in your mealtime." "Your child is suffering from a need to control." Yet, "Take your child's recovery out of her hands."

What we didn't know was that we were in the dark through the darkest days. We were led to believe that her stay would be a mere two days. Of course, it seems foolish to us now that we would ever think that. We were not even granted a meeting with the psychiatrist to discuss Jenna's situation until the third day, Wednesday, at which time it appeared to us that the automatic sequence for every patient is long-term hospitalization. As Tom and I sat huddled on cold, hard, folding chairs in a tiny conference room, we listened to her evaluation team share their observations and conclusions regarding Jenna's "obvious sense of denial" about her anorexic behavior.

First was Dr. Singer, director of the center, whose kind eyes spoke more than his words ever could. In his late fifties, conservatively dressed, suit a bit rumpled, he seemed to have avoided the usual ego path of many such professionals.

Not so, Dr. Newman, a GQ-dressed psychiatrist who always seemed to look just past us or over us, never truly at us. Lots of talking, but superficial listening. He's heard it all before. Doesn't really need to acknowlege this family's story. I kept noticing him glancing down at his watch. Time is money.

Next sat Germaine, nutritionist, with her coal black, long curly hair and bohemian way of dress and manner. She wore long, flowing skirts, each a vivid textural tribute to one or another exotic culture, fringed vests, and beaded chains, bracelets and earrings, and no make-up. When she spoke, it was with the forceful yet "cool" attitude of someone who's been there and can relate to the young population she worked with. In fact, many of the staff members were survivors of eating disorders themselves. Jenna came to adore Germaine and all her avant-garde style.

Then there was the dietician, Janice. Swelling with eighth-month belly of baby, she paraded proudly in bright, Andy Warhol-inspired knit outfits of polka-dots and pop-art in fuscia, turquoise and neon green. Her long, acrylic nails always sported a different painted pattern, crescent moons, hearts, Phoenix Suns logo. A recovered anorexic herself, when she spoke, she scared the hell out of me. Cold, demanding, intimidating. Wouldn't want to mess with Janice. It was she who took command of our meeting as she sternly concluded that Jenna would, of course, remain hospitalized. We were told, not asked. Why couldn't I see this coming? I felt control slipping away as I tried hard to trust the system.

"...and so, Mr. and Mrs. Foster, as you can see, Jenna clearly needs round-the-clock supervision and therapy. Paramount to us is getting Jenna's weight up," Janice droned on.

My eyes glazed over, as I tried to decode these unfamiliar phrases. "I see. Okay, now what?"

"We review each case every Wednesday. We will meet with you again next week."

The team of four abruptly stood and left the cubicle. Tom and I just sat there, feeling awkward and abandoned. We next had to tell Jenna, whom we found sitting expectantly on her bed. She assumed she'd be going home with us after the meeting. Tom tried to gently explain what we had just been told. Jenna sat stunned with a look of contempt for me that I had betrayed her, tricked her into indefinite committment. It took work on my part to convince her that we were just as ill-informed and surprised as she that she was not coming home.

"Jenna, honey," I spoke softly when we found ourselves leaving her for a second time, "it will be all right. Everything will be okay. We need to trust these people. They know what they're doing and they're here to help you. Please do your part to get well, and we'll do ours. You are so very important to us all. You'll be home again soon, I promise." Oops, I shouldn't say that. I don't know a damned thing anymore.

We left her that night, she looking sadder than ever.

Once home, I fell into bed, journal and pen in hand, and struggled to give words to my emotions.

Mother's Journal Entry

You have no idea. It is most like standing in a pitch dark closet. A grave enemy, a monster is coming at me. I don't know from what direction. Danger, danger. Terror. I keep striking out in the black. I feel nothing out there, but it's real. Formless and life-threatening. Total fear and vulnerability. I have never, ever felt such day-to-day terror, moment-to-moment despair while I go on with my routines. I cry at any time. I feel so alone. I am the mother. I am Mother, like never before. I sign all the many forms for hospitalization, and below my signature, "MOTHER." Mother. I am the mother. This is my child, my daughter, my only daughter, my beautiful girl. I cannot lose her. Why is she starving herself? Why? What the hell happened?

Jenna's Journal

August 30

I can't understand
why I'm here
People are moaning "ouch"
while the staff checks for lice
They stare blankly
with hopeless eyes
They smell bad
They're here because
they cry too much
or they yell too much
or they hear voices
or they were touched too much
or not enough
or they tried to end it
or they tried to abuse it

But I didn't.
I shouldn't be here.
It's too cold here and I didn't bring a sweatshirt.
I can't talk to my friends
or make phone calls
or even have a bag not locked up.
They all keep saying how they "understand"
how I'm "frustrated."

But they don't.

As our family struggled to find our footing in this new circumstance of Jenna's hospitalization, we had to adapt to new rules and etiquette, the dance steps of a re-defined "normal." We were aliens in a new land, fully immersed in a new language: Clinical Case Manager, Psych Tech, COR Nurse, Utilization Management Nurse, aftercare, intake, staffing, C.D. (chemical dependency), and on and on. Rules for visitation were carefully laid out and stringently followed. Only parents were allowed in. This left all three siblings lonely and feeling cut off from each other. Tom and I were required to obtain a stamped and dated visitor's badge at the front reception desk, and any items brought in for a patient were checked by staff at the nurses' station before being given to the inmate – er, patient. No outside visits or trips were allowed. Patients were permitted to call parents only, and strictly from 5:15-6:00 p.m., with a staff member dialing the number and monitoring the call.

Every night at six o'clock, either alone or with Tom, I knocked on the locked ward to be let in to Jenna's stark room. She sat on the edge of her bed, clutching Poppyseed in a visible struggle to know the right thing to say or do. I tried to make a little small talk at first, then asked about her day. We each stumbled around the rhythm of conversation. At precisely eight-thirty our visit had to end, and I hugged my daughter and walked out, hearing the doors lock behind me.

During our first few visits, Jenna said very little, giving me one word answers to my questions or berating me for duping her into being there. By the third or fourth day she began to respond to my visits with visible gratitude that I was there. Her mood lifted whenever I walked in, and I could almost see her body exhale the longer I was there, until the inevitable dread of my leaving again came around. Sometimes we talked a lot; sometimes we talked little. Sometimes we talked about the "thing"; sometimes we just couldn't. She often spoke about the other teens in the hospital, always stunned by the degree of dysfunction in their lives.

"Mom, these kids are really messed up. And you wouldn't believe their parents. Some don't even come to visit." Jenna had led a normal, peaceful, and healthy life up until now. The only serious crisis had been her parents' divorce, and even that had never been violent or abusive. She was certainly getting a crash course in Fucked-up Families 101. What was she doing here? How was our own family fucked up? Or was it? Or isn't everybody's to some degree?

Willow Creek's highly touted program (as that of many other eating disorder clinics) was based on a combination of behavior modification, group counseling, education on nutrition and physiology, and medication where warranted. Patients followed rigid protocol governing their eating. Each patient was assigned a staff member who carefully monitored all food eaten. No visitors were permitted during meals. Overuse of ice was not permitted. No caffeinated beverages. Mealtimes were precisely thirty minutes; any uneaten food after that time was considered calories which had to be made up for by drinking the dietary supplement Ensure™ within fifteen minutes. The staff's frequent refrain was, "We must first sustain the patient physically, before therapy can help." Several times when Jenna just couldn't force herself to eat every bite at all three meals in a day, an overwhelming task, her staff aide insisted on her consuming the tiny Ensure™ can. She hated that, and would still be in tears retelling me in the evening. But she understood that if she refused, her admittance to the program would be terminated, and I saw her complying as a shred of her willingness to accept treatment.

Patients were weighed every morning with careful attention paid to preventing any cheating of the scales. Patients were weighed shoeless and backwards, and not told their weight so that they could not assess their own success at starving and modify accordingly. Trips to the bathroom throughout the day were monitored to detect any bulimic activity, and as part of the psychiatric ward dictate, residents and their belongings were carefully inspected regularly for any number of contraband items, particularly those that could be used for self-destructive purposes.

Jenna's tightly scheduled days included sessions on goal-setting, study time, recreation, crafts, social skills, self-development, health and wellness. During one craft session, patients braided "friendship bracelets," and were encouraged to exchange with another resident. Jenna had struck a bond with young girl named Audrey, and on one of my visits, proudly displayed the bracelet Audrey had made for her.

"I'm never going to take this off! I'm going to wear it till it drops off." *Oh God,* I thought, *this will only happen when you've lost enough more weight.*

Patients posted nutrition charts they made, along with construction paper collages of magazine cutouts that they felt expressed how they saw themselves. The walls looked like elementary school rooms. Lights out at 8:30. Every minute of every day was structured and supervised.

Weekends, however, were the worst.

During the week, every minute of her day was scheduled, assigned, and monitored. But come Saturday and Sunday there were no counseling or group sessions, no planned activities at all. Those sixty or so hours from Friday evening to Monday morning loomed long and dismal to Jenna as she fought boredom and forced herself to mingle with the others confined for a multitude of reasons. So, on the weekends I tried to stay three or four hours. I brought Rummicube, cards, or other games to play to move us beyond small talk. One afternoon Tom, Jenna, and I started singing The Statler Brothers' "Flowers on the Wall." "Countin' flowers on the wall, that don't bother me at all. Playin' Solitaire till dawn with a deck of fifty-one. Smokin' cigarettes and watchin' Captain Kangaroo, now don't tell me... I've nothin' to do." We laughed and laughed, painfully aware of how well that described the loneliness of her long, empty weekend. I still vividly recall the dumbfounded looks on her fellow residents' faces when we opened her door to leave after that wonderful afternoon visit, as they tried to sort out how a teen and her parents could have such fun together.

Mother's Journal Entry

Thursday – Your first smile in seeing me. Great visit. Irish jokes. laugh a lot, smile a lot. You hold my hand and reassure me. I am encouraged. It's the first time in awhile I haven't been afraid you were going to die.

Friday – Tom visits you alone. Brings you three pink roses. High school buddies, Kerri and

> Vince, come by the house with a card for you and questions for me. We have a lovely visit for an hour. They leave feeling much better. You have great friends.
>
> Saturday – A long afternoon's visit. That night you spoke to Greg on the phone, "I'll be home before you know it, back on the school bus with you." Greg, in the naked embarrassment of a fourteen year-old, quietly sobbed.

Group therapy sessions were not productive for our daughter. But Jenna is a quick study, clever in working a situation, so after one week there, she was sure she had "seen the light," understood so much about nutrition and the body, actually thanked me for the whole experience and was confident that she could handle her recovery and that now she could come home. With the hope that love demands, I tried to believe her.

Back again for another Wednesday's meeting with the staff to evaulate "the patient's progress and determination of release." I prayed for good news and an end to this nightmarish routine. I felt confident Jenna's counselors would be as moved as I was at how quickly she seemed to understand the gravity of her behavior. Now my girl could come home. I had even alerted Greg to make a Welcome Home sign.

We expected an in-depth discussion on Jenna's state of mind and body. Instead, the staffing was a disaster. Dr. Newman sailed in twelve minutes late, sat with us for fifteen minutes, with Janice in attendance, and as I was speaking in mid-sentence, he stood up and cut me off, declaring that he had already given us more time than he could allow. Janice dismissed us with, "Jenna is still in full denial." And at eighty-five pounds, she could not be released. Jenna was crushed when we told her. My heart broke as we cried together. *Hang on, baby, hang on.*

Dejected, Tom and I arrived home that night, and as I plodded up the stairs I felt all life drain out of my legs in collapse. With Tom behind me, I looked to the top of the stairs to see Nathan and Greg. Someone must have asked me about some household chore I hadn't tended to, because in the next moment, I screamed at my three males for expecting the house to still be run as smoothly and all too solely by me. I cannot remember ever verbally attacking them all like that before, or since. I yelled in the rageful voice of one who fears no one can hear her; who thinks that if she is loud enough, all the gods will finally, finally answer. I wasn't really yelling about the house at all. But suddenly, Tom, Nathan, and Greg seemed like annoying pets in the house that just kept needing me without giving much slack in return.

I felt broken down as never before. With looks of helpless confusion, my three men just stared silently at me. Me, the Mother.

When we were first facing hospitalization and an undetermined number of days that Jenna-Marie would be missing school, we had to meet with her school counselor. Tom and I had to be in our own classrooms by 8:00, so Ms. Le Roy, an attractive, slim forty-five-year-old, met us at the door of her office one morning at 7:15. Jenna's teachers were also there to discuss possible long-term consequences of her extended absence. We sat in a small conference room where the six teachers, gradebooks in hands, greeted us with sympathetic smiles. So many times I had been where they were sitting. So many parent conferences I had been called upon to speak kindly and diplomatically about one's son or daughter as I studied for clues from the parents as to why their child was the way he or she was. So often had Tom and I been asked to bend the rules and expectations for students in special circumstances. Now we were the parents with those pleading looks on our faces. *Please care about our girl. Please have mercy for this student, our daughter.* It felt so odd to be sitting on the parent side this time. I fought back tears of embarrassment and desperation, but found comfort in the familiarity of knowing some of these people. One teacher was the son of my former principal. Another was the daughter of one of my own colleagues. We don't live in a small town, but the circular communities of educators often intersect.

Diane deftly reviewed the situation we were most likely facing with Jenna missing who-knows-how-many days of school ahead, then led discussion around the table as each teacher explained Jenna's academic progress at only five weeks into the year.

English – "Jenna is a lovely girl who has been writing exemplary papers on Shakespeare. She has a 95% right now. She could do the reading on her own in the hospital. I understand her friend Marie is in the same class; I could give her the work."

Government – "At the start of the year, Jenna participated each day and worked well in small groups. Lately I've seen her sort of retreat into a sad silence. Her current grade is a B. I'll make up some study guides to help her while she is out."

Drama – "Of course, you know we all love Jenna in drama. We've worked with her for three years now and are hoping to have her direct a senior play in the spring. Tell her we miss her terribly."

Psychology – "I like Jenna very much. I have certainly noticed the physical and emotional signs of her disorder and been very concerned. She strikes me as a remarkable young lady who is fighting this battle hard. After two chapter tests,

Jenna has a 90% and all of her work in, but missing too many days will definitely set her back. I can write out the chapter outlines in advance for her."

Physics – "Jenna is such a bright young lady, and like the others, I've been worried about her. She is getting her work in, but her test scores are slipping. This is a high-powered course and she simply cannot miss more than a few days in class. I would hate to see her have to drop. Let's see what we can do."

Math – "Jenna is a delightful girl who tries to help others in class. Frankly, Mr. and Mrs. Foster, this is Trigonometry, a higher level math, however, and if she misses more than a few days, her grade will definitely be threatened. Perhaps she could work with a tutor; I'll prepare some worksheets for her."

I squeezed Tom's hand under the table as I looked around at all these educators' compassionate faces. My heart was filled with gratitude. We tried to take in all the extra efforts they were willing to go to for our daughter. She was just another one of their students, yet everyone in the room appreciated the gravity of our situation and treated it with dignity. My years of compassion and dedication toward other parents' sons and daughters were being repaid to me a hundredfold by fellow professionals who now truly cared for this, and every, student.

Finally, Tom and I stood and reached across the table to shake every teacher's hand, thanking each for such extraordinary measures and communal support. As we left the conference room with them still sitting around the table, I could almost feel their bowed heads slowly shaking in shared frustration, hear their muffled voices of concern.

During Jenna's second week of hospitalization, she was much less resistant to therapy. I knew this was progress, but as routine and passive acceptance set in, I could see her strong spirit turning to submissiveness, and I worried that the best of her personality was changing. Her curiosity about life, and her openness to experiencing all it has to offer, seemed to dissolve before my eyes. She simply did not care much about anything.

But she was eating. This thousand-dollar-a-day program was all about weight, and with our insurance covering it only on a week-by-week appeal, in-house treatment was conditional. They could not keep a patient once he or she reached a certain number on the scale, whatever they determined as a reasonable weight for maintaining life, regardless of any real progress mentally or emotionally. So after two weeks, when Jenna's weight, albeit under their control, was up to ninty-two pounds, she was released.

Jenna's Journal

September 14

I have so much that I want to remember from the Willow Creek experience. Here's a bit:

1. First night and with no sweatshirt! Pizza and movies and all the rules.

2. Bill, the attendant – those teeth, that creepy smile, long nails and glazed eyes…(shudder)

3. Danielle and the "Look of Doom"—while she was on suicide alert, she became my roommate. So you can imagine my terror when I decided to have an apple but got a phone call and had to leave it, and returned to find my knife missing.

Thank God it was just Dana who took it away.

4. Hairy, aren't I?

5. The first meal I had—fried chicken and fried zucchini…how traumatized can I possibly get?

6. Each day's Round Table: High point of the day? Low point?

7. The ultimate rude awakening: 7:00 a.m., blinding white light suddenly in my eyes, and an immense woman looming above me, shoving a needle into my arm to take blood.

8. The gecko above my bed one morning.

9. Doris asking me every single morning if I still had gowns to be weighed in.

10. Bathroom being locked/no alone time for two hours after I've eaten.

11. Being not one, but two people's high point this last Saturday—feels like I'm me again.

12. Okay, roommates who have come and gone: Lori, Liz, Danielle, Theresa, Christie, Marta, Ruthie. Seven! I never even shared a bedroom in my life before this.

13. Realizing that each meal is like Christmas—and should be cherished just as much.

September 18

Today was a pretty "normal" (I use the term lightly) day at the hospital until my parents came in for a family session and after that, they had a staffing with my doctor. Then my doctor told me that I could be discharged! But with "grave reservations" and only because Janice

> recommended it. Dr. Singer didn't want to at first because I've lost weight (probably playing that basketball game—oh, hell it was worth it), so I'll just have to eat all my meals and try not to exercise (easier said than done). So at dinner I had way too much for my tastes, but I can't do anything about that right now. I just have to be able to recognize what's my tastes and what's the E.D.'s tastes. But anyway… So I came home!!!!
>
> I talked to Marie, Jenn, and Vince and got caught up on the latest gossip, and left a message on Kerri's machine. It feels so good to be *HOME.*

On Monday, September 14, Jenna was released from residential treatment. I was so grateful to have her back in the loving arms of our family, but I felt no joy. Something in me was holding me back. Perhaps it was because the doctor let her go with "great reservations"; the words burned in my brain. Perhaps it was because Jenna was extremely agitated from medication and difficult to even approach. Perhaps it was because I was now going to a new unknown—Life at Home After… —and old fears were reawakening. *How much will fall to me now to "fix?"* I pushed thoughts away, not allowing myself to process it all because I had to hold up for the time being. If I think, if I feel too much, I'll fall apart, and I'm so tired of crying.

Jenna's closest friends came by that evening to welcome her back. As she opened the door, everyone was screaming in adolescent excitement. I watched from the top of the stairs. They devoured Jenna in a group hug so tight it seemed she'd burst. "She's fragile!" I wanted to cry out. But I just leaned over the upstairs ledge and took it all in, smiling. There was sweet music in our home that night.

Maybe this was over, I thought. But in a room of wellness, illness still resided.

Jenna's Journal

September 21

> The last week has been an emotional roller coaster. I don't want to be here, but I don't want to be at the hospital, but I don't want to miss anything here, but I miss the "safety" of the hospital. Maybe I just can't deal with living the two separate lives—I need one or the other.

What do people without insurance do when life has tossed them willy-nilly into a crisis that forces a price tag on recovery? Where do they turn? The exorbitant rate of this and most other facilities prohibits those without resources from getting the help they need and deserve. And how do parents who live far distances from help continue to be there for their children? How do they maintain their jobs and routines? To whom do they go for respite? How lucky we were. Matters of transportation, time, and paperwork were mere irritants when compared with parents dealing with far worse on a daily basis for years on end. Each time Jenna was recommended for in-house treatment, I feared this might be the time our insurance company would say no. Then what?

A condition of Jenna's release from Willow Creek was that she continue on an all-day outpatient basis with regular weigh-ins under their supervision. Were her weight to go down again, re-admittance would take place. She was also expected to follow up with a counselor of her choice.

Unfortunately, she had merely learned the game quickly and gone through the motions of recovery to get back home. Jenna was certainly not yet equipped to reenter so-called normal life, and within a week she was losing weight and found herself referred back in for residential treatment. This was crushing. By now everyone was telling me that nothing to do with an eating disorder was a quick fix, to hunker down for the long haul. Yes, I could feel it beginning. I had no idea, however, what "it" was.

So back to Willow Creek. Again we packed the duffel bag. Again we walked down the diagonal courtyard, greeted the orderlies, were led through locked doors, tried not to look too closely at the stares of the other troubled teens (new faces, same expressions) and settled our daughter in to a new room. Jenna's second hospitalization took on a different tone for me. During her first go around of residential treatment, I visited her every evening, exacting a terrible toll on the rest of our home life and my work. Every aspect of my life, outside of Jenna, was being neglected. Laundry to do, bills to pay, lessons to plan, mom to call, dinners to cook, sons and husband to love. Even as I moved zombie-like through the motions, I felt I was failing everyone. *Ignore your exhaustion; must keep the plates spinning.*

This time I felt a bit angry, and wondered if my disproportional attention wasn't even enabling my daughter's behavior. As I stood in this room going through the usual mom-motions, my voice began speaking without my even thinking, and it felt heavy with authenticity. I sat my girl down on the worn pink and yellow daisy bedspread and spoke in a sobering voice.

"Jenna, I told you back in July that you were preventing me from doing my essential job of nourishing you. I was wrong. It is not my job anymore; it's your job as a young adult.

You're going to be eighteen in a few weeks; you must be in charge of you, of taking good care of the life God has given you. It's now your responsibility to nourish yourself."

She hung her head, matted hair covering her face, and dug her fingers into the sculpted patterns of chenille.

"Honey, look at me."

She would not, but our dynamic changed in that moment as my daughter and I began the move into an adult-adult dance. For me, it was liberating. *Mother* does not cause everything and cannot fix everything... and should not. This felt like such a gamble, yet I spoke with conviction, and as the very words tumbled out, I knew they were exactly right.

Healing comes from within. It is self-empowering or it is transient.

I tried to continue.

"I'm still here by your side. I will never leave you. But you have work to do here. You are the major player and recovery will come as you let it. Learn from what is being put in front of you. Listen to those all around you who are here to help. I'll do it with you, but I cannot do it for you or even to you." I leaned in close to her face. "Can you understand this?"

Jenna never said a word, but nodded ever so slightly.

"Do the work."

I stood up, kissed the top of her head, and left the room, walked through the wing, crossed the courtyard, retraced the lobby, and found the parking lot. Numbed, I did not feel the ground beneath me. *Trust*, I kept telling myself. *Trust in yourself. In your daughter. In God Almighty. Because that's all you have.*

Chapter Six

Eighty Pounds

I left Jenna with a lot to think about that night. I gave her several days without a visit to get serious and think about this thing. She needed time alone to come to grips with her self-recovery.

This monstrous disease, this evil that had grabbed hold of my girl and turned her inside out, and our lives upside down, was foreign to me. I didn't recognize its shape. I barely spoke its language. I needed to get to know it better. So I took a self-guided crash course into the world of anorexia nervosa. This is where the dark rabbit hole of online research can suffocate one's time and energy. Today's social media also makes it far too easy for sufferers of this mental illness to form alliances and networks, feeding their very disease. Most horrifying are the "pro-anorexia" sites that actually provide tips on how to destroy oneself in the name of thinness, even personifying their demons by bestowing not-so-cute nicknames on their disease, like *Anna* or *Rexie*, (anorexia) or *Edie* (eating disorder).

I drowned in cyber-pools of information, clinging to parent testimonies for hope, only to learn of many families that battle this demon for years, sometimes only to lose in the end. *We will be different*, I railed in defiance. But doesn't every family think so? Hundreds of articles and websites floated across my computer screen, but few spoke of recovery, and even fewer from a parent's vantage point. What I most related to was the utter waste of blame, no matter where it is placed, because every parent carries around a heavy box of blame that seems to have no end to how much it can hold. It is insidious. Society blames the parents and victims. Parents blame themselves. Victims blame themselves. Parents blame society. But blame serves no purpose, accomplishes no goal. *Blame*, and its partner, *guilt*, divert us from the concentrated effort and supreme strength needed in this war. If I were to be any good to my child, if I were to be of any substantial help, I must choose to not spend my energies and emotions on self-blame or self-pity. Such waste those are. Fruitless, too, is the time we spend laying guilt at the feet of others. Jenna? Her father? Society? Peers? A thousand years of feminine history? The questioning has never ended for me, even to this day, but to focus on indicting one or another cheats everyone out of the one hundred percent effort required to survive crises like this one.

Soon I had to break away from my addictive late-night routine of cyber research. The personal websites read self-defeating and theatrical. What was I supposed to do with this information, anyway? I always came away feeling worse and understanding less. I wasn't sure I wanted to chat online with other parents in the same situation. After all, no two parents are in exactly the same circumstances. This would not be my lifeline. I needed to hear from a parent who was winning! Most of all, I ached for a step-by-step, do-it-yourself blueprint to heal my daughter.

Of course, such a thing does not exist. But I did learn much about the physiological costs of starvation, self-induced or not. How, once the body's protective fat disappears, along with it goes the protein structure of organs and muscles, leaving the body to eventually waste away. How victims risk a greater incidence of heart attack, edema, liver failure, osteoporosis. The body is a fascinating, brilliant machine programmed for one thing: survival. Ironically, in its desperate need for sustenance, the body actually begins to cannibalize itself to postpone its own demise. Skin becomes dry and raw, hair thins and falls out, nails split, teeth decay, and menstruation is altered. Victims often develop what's called *lanugo*, a soft, downy hair all over the body, which is its way of maintaining warmth. I pored over reports on the mental degradation one can expect: the loss of concentration and sustained eye contact, diminished intellect and mental alertness.

The Land of Eating Disorders had opened up before me, and as I pored over the latest research, I realized that first someone out there must understand my daughter, then I will be able to arm myself with the proper weaponry. Since Jenna did not fit many of the assumed traits of anorexics, I dug deep to find the category she did belong in. Eventually I found it. A number of clinicians note the perfectionist drive that many anorexics exhibit. They may feel an obsession to succeed, to answer all needs of others, and when life's setbacks befall their loved ones, as life will naturally do, they can feel like failures. They may be misguided into thinking that they have disappointed those who mean the most to them. Such destructive mental messages begin to form in the dark where there are no words.

Do we not all have that voice inside, those words and tapes that sneak into our consciousness to undo us? Tapes from moms and dads, tapes from our insecurities, tapes from past insults. "I look fat." "I won't get that job." "He could never love me." "I'll bet they're talking about me." "I always do everything wrong." "I am a failure, a fraud at life." Every day we choose to listen to either the negative or positive voice. Which will we empower? Which will rule us? In the mind of the anorexic, she does not deserve reward, nourishment, inner peace, food, so self-denial becomes its just compensation, in a sense.

Was this Jenna? If so, why now, just when all was starting to fall into place for our family? Why at all? I grew weary of asking why.

Defeating the negative mind lies in essentially drowning it in the positive. I thought of the old Cherokee parable about the young boy who is tormented between two wolves inside his head. One is evil; the other is good. When the boy asks his grandfather, the chief, "Which wolf will win?" the old man replies, "The one you feed."

I knew I had to feed the positive mind and starve the negative. I had to reassure Jenna that it was not her job to keep Mom or anyone else happy or free from the struggles that come with living. And when only the verbal venom of the negative mind was spewing out of her mouth, I had to somehow listen to what she wasn't saying.

This finally is something I can do. I may not have all the psychological expertise in counseling; I may make mistakes in how to deal with moments at the dinner table. But love my Jenna, I could. I was an expert at that. So I began a routine I follow to this day: I write love letters to my daughter. I decided that these would demonstrate unconditional love and acceptance and devotion from me to her, parent to child. I love her when she is beautiful, I love her when she looks horrible. I love her when she is well and when she is ill. I love her when she eats; I love her when she does not. I love her when she is sweet, loving, fun, accommodating and hopeful. But I also love her when the clutching hooks of depression, remoteness, stubbornness, and resentment lash out from her to everyone. I will take her on her own terms, always. That is love. I do not have to like her to love her or stay devoted to her. It will not go away.

I had to face what "unconditional" means. How rarely we speak it to those who need it most. We parents must not just feel love or show love when our children are pretty, achieving, or obedient. We must not only accept them when they become what we want or follow paths we wish we had.

And while the spoken word can be sweet sounds, there is something magical about the written message. You can hold my words in your hand forever. You can see my personality within the slants and curlicues of my labored handwriting. You can read it over and over and over again without any tarnish of time or distortion of wording. You can hide it in a secret box, or frame it for the world to see. The written word, simple black ink on white paper, has a certain quality of infinity to it.

I bought a softbound journal that offered an inspirational quote on both sides of each page. Somehow I always managed to find a page with just the right message I was looking for on that day to penetrate her diseased emotional shell. I tried to neatly tear each one out from a binding that wasn't designed for tearing. Jagged, messy rip. But soon I accepted how imperfectly each tore, and realized the very perfection of imperfection. We're not leading perforated lives either, and this brought me a strange reassurance. In these letters, I never spoke of the disorder, never mentioned any problems or concerns or even news. I wanted them to take on a sort of timelessness. The letters were to be pure gifts of love, hope, faith and spirit. No fear. I slipped one into her hand as I left the hospital each night I visited. Though she never said it, I could sense their growing importance to her. Neither of us spoke of the letters, but as she received each one from me, I caught, in those distant eyes, the slightest look of relief that I had not forgotten that night.

I didn't know if my words were helping; I was sometimes afraid they would sound cheesy or simplistic or inarticulate, or repetitious—a writing teacher is her own worst critic. But I was not writing to be applauded. They couldn't hurt, I reasoned, and I thought about how I would feel reading such words of love. Later, when she returned home, I continued to place a letter on her bed pillow when she'd least expect it. She told me much later that they always seemed to be "delivered" when she most needed it.

Jenna soon adopted the rhythm of love-writing and left me notes or letters of reciprocal expressions, coming only from the positive mind. Sometimes as brief as "Thank you," or "I'm O.K.," other times long litanies of devotion, she always closed her poetic notes to her mother with "I love you from the ground to God." What she put into writing seemed to come from a voice deep within her that was hiding for a time, a voice that said what she often couldn't aloud. It was my real daughter in there, not the twisted, malformed being taking up her space, what there was left of it. She was in there. Jenna was still in there, my sweet little girl who was working very hard to hang on as gales of fear and chaos pulled at her fragile form.

Day after day of hospitalization changed my daughter. Still losing weight, now at eighty pounds, she was almost evaportating before my eyes. Emaciated, with eyes sunken, hair unwashed and unkempt, she was almost unrecognizable. She wore only her shabbiest clothes, and she now took on the fixation of constant motion with her legs. She would sit, legs crossed, and swing her leg unceasingly, almost violently. In fact, from the moment she woke each day until her body finally gave in to sleep at night, Jenna's legs were moving. Leg swinging, or foot tapping, or body swaying. Constant. Constant. Constant. My daughter continued this nonstop for nearly three months! I don't know how she did it, how she could physically maintain such exertion. It drove us all crazy, but I tried to say nothing, for when I did she would lash out at me saying that she couldn't help it. I took to standing in her bedroom after she was asleep just to look at her little body in the temporary peace of blessed stillness as she slept. It brought me relief.

The clinic blamed her obsessive behavior on medication, or her attempt at exercise to burn calories, explaining that many anorexics concoct the most bizarre strategies to lose more pounds.

Jenna's exterior self was simply a manifestation of her inner deterioration, however. My daughter's entire personality, her very spirit, had vanished, being replaced by this unrecognizable young thing, abysmally despondent, sullen, and hopeless. I wondered, was depression simply manifesting itself in starvation, or did the starvation of the brain lead to depression? I was long past the naïve thinking that the key to her recovery, the solution to this problem, was simply to eat.

She spoke often of her depression, blaming the clinic and its rigid, stifling structure for killing her love of life. She could sense herself drifting away from caring about anything. Through our long winter of disorder, my terror came from the possibility of her dying, but my sadness, an overpowering grief at times, came from what seemed like the dying of her spirit. I wanted to save her life, spirit intact. All her life I had never known Jenna to waver from an abundant, irrepressible joy in living. She was always curious about everything, willing to try anything. She carried great compassion for others and a deep spirituality and faith. All of that seemed to fall away. Eating disorders are a slow suicide. That plagued me most of all. Why would my daughter want to destroy herself?

Mother's Journal Entry

A lonely spot lies in the core of the
heart of a mother.
It is the loneliest spot on earth.
This spot is tiny, yet deep,
  dark and long
          and silent
Within it the mother sits all alone
Alone with her fears
          her joys
          her memories
All which none may know or touch.
She can express rightly to no one.
Only another mother may smile, knowingly,
yet even she cannot know.
No one can go to the spot—it is too small
          and silent —
for anyone to find.
  But it is there.
And within it, Mother is alone.
          How lonely a place is Mother.
Who would have known?

I am coated. I am so coated with a film that shields me. The worse things get, the thicker my coat, for if I let down I will crumble into a heap of dry leaves.

I maintain.

I manage home and work and try to take good care of Greg, especially, since he was the youngest.

I am coated. I do not think—I cannot. I do not feel—I dare not, or I sense I would die.

I act.

My greatest fear is so unspeakable that, were I to draw it up from the bowels of my heart, it would lodge in my throat, suffocating my breath.

Willow Creek recommended to parents that they attend the facility's weekly family therapy sessions. Every Wednesday afternoon, Tom and I arrived and were asked to wait in the lobby for the residents to come back from lunch. In they'd walk in single file like some sort of grotesque patient parade. Some with feeding tubes, some hunched over like elderly-trapped-in-teenager, some looking like moving twigs. But no one ever appeared engaged in the moment; each seemed completely remote. It was heartbreaking to see young people in even worse shape than Jenna, those who had battled this for years, those who had a multitude of psychological disorders, those from severely dysfunctional families like the young woman who wanted never to see her mother again.

There was Timmy, a fourteen-year-old boy who sat with his grossly obese mother who wouldn't let him finish a sentence. Timmy was on a feeding tube, which is a particularly uncomfortable and humiliating state to reach when one just refuses food or drink. He had been in and out of treatment for three years.

There was Alan, nineteen, who held hands with his thirty-year-old lover/guardian, Sergio, striking a practiced sensei pose.

And Sarah, the one whose mother never showed up because if she did, "I'll kill her with a pair of scissors, I swear." With a body that revealed the ravages of fifteen years of battling with starvation, Sarah had been through several residential treatment programs from Colorado to Vermont, and looked far older than her twenty-six years.

The saddest was Yvonne, sixteen, who was taller and thinner than Jenna, I estimated. I could not fathom what was holding her body up or keeping her breath going; she looked like walking string. Yvonne had attempted suicide three times.

We left each meeting feeling no more enlightened or even understood. No bonding between parents took place, and we certainly didn't go out afterward for a beer. Each seemed lost in his or her own painful embarrassment at being there. Yet strangely, we did share something significant. We were all mother and father figures in the torturous throes of fighting for a loved one. Jenna, also needed not to dwell on any similarity or difference she felt with the other patients. It just did not matter. Her life was her life.

After each meeting, Tom and I would walk with Jenna back to her room for a brief private visit before we left, and those in her wing, residents and employees alike, seemed almost taken aback by the affection and lightness between us three. I'm sure we looked pretty goofy. While our distinction from the rest of the patient community validated me as a parent, it only added to my anguish in trying to determine a cause for our nightmare.

One afternoon, a staff member took me aside and told me that there seemed to emerge some tiny hints to a possible experience of assault or abuse upon my daughter. The very thought turned me inside out. But Jenna adamantly denied this over and over, and no theory ever really took a clear shape. At one of our individual staffings, I implored her clinicians to magically hand us answers. Tell me what I did wrong. Tell me what I am doing wrong, for God's sake; I can take it! We were told we may never know the root, and that that should not hinder recovery. This gave me some relief, but to this day I will still unconsciously allow a silent one-word question to seep into my day's thoughts now and then: *Why?*

But there was mention at one of our staff meetings about the baffling lack of any serious issue in our family. The psychiatrists and aides noted the unusually close relationship between Jenna and me and felt perhaps this was a clue. As she was approaching her last year of high school with the adult world looming, Jenna seemed to cling to her childhood, exhibiting little girl behaviors. Perhaps very deep in her subconscious, by not eating and thereby retarding her growth, she could halt the natural progression away from me. How ironic. I had worked hard to have a healthy, close mother-daughter relationship beyond what I ever had with my mother, and it may be contributing to this horrid ailment. We foolish, well-intentioned gamblers.

On a Saturday afternoon, as I was leaving after an hours-long visit, I stopped at the hospital's cafeteria for a cold drink. As I sat there, I noticed a woman sitting nearby, and recognized her as one of the mothers in our family sessions. She looked my way and offered me a sad and knowing smile. She walked over to me and politely asked to speak with me.

"Of course," I said. "Please join me."

She sat down on the edge of the hard, plastic chair. "My name is Carol. My daughter's name is Theresa. She's the one with the extremely short black hair." She spoke slowly and with caution. An attractive woman, about my age, Carol had soft, grey eyes fringed with laugh lines and cry lines. She was professionally dressed and meticulously mannered.

"Oh, yes, of course. I'm Valerie."

"Your daughter, it's Jenna isn't it, started here around the same time my Theresa did, I think." Carol seemed to struggle for her words. "I hope you don't mind my assertiveness here, but I've watched you in our meetings and I feel I can trust you. I just need someone to talk to and I wonder if we couldn't meet some time, just to maybe help each other, mother to mother?"

"I guess so." What else could one say? "Would you like to go somewhere now?" I offered.

"No, I can't. I have to pick up my son from soccer practice. But how about Monday or Tuesday?" She began to fidget, car keys in hand.

"Well, I usually get here for my visit around six o'clock. We could meet nearby for a cup of coffee before that."

"Oh, yes, that would be nice."

"Where would you like to meet?"

"Oh, I don't know. We are new here in the valley, and I don't know my way around yet." She was now standing nervously.

I wracked my brain to quickly settle on a location, since I, too, was feeling a bit uncomfortable and wanted this scene settled.

"There's a cafe just a couple of blocks from here at the next light, on the northwest corner. How about we meet there at five o'clock on Monday?" *What am I doing?*, I thought to myself.

"Oh, that would be lovely. Thank you so much." She grasped my hand in her two; they were cold.

She walked away looking tired, with the posture of a woman much older than she was.

By the time Monday afternoon rolled around, I was running late from school, weaving in and out of sluggish rush-hour traffic and regretting having made arrangements to meet this woman. *I don't even know her*, I rationalized to myself. *I don't have time for this. But she seems to need it so; I can't say no to another mother. Maybe this will be good for me, too. Oh well, we'll just see. It's only an hour.*

I got to the cafe at just after five and didn't see her anywhere. *Maybe she cancelled and I can just have a quick bite to eat in peace.*

In she walked.

"Hi, Valerie."

"Hello, Carol. It's nice to see you again," I said, and strangely meant it. "Carol, I have to eat something. Can I get you a sandwich?"

"Oh no, thanks, I have to cook dinner later for my family. I'll eat then."

"O.K."

For the next hour we sat and exchanged stories, mom to mom. She traced her own devastating years' history of Theresa's battles with alcholism, anorexia, even bulimia. How her daughter had run away from home several times, been in and out of several residential treatment programs, and had attempted suicide more than once. By now, Carol and her family were on the verge of bankruptcy and a no-way-back depletion of emotional reserves.

"My daughter just seems to be trying to figure out who she is, but can't. We've gone through the name change phase, when she told us we were to only call her Terri, then it was Tres, than just T. What kind of name is that? But we did it. Then it was the hair, which kept getting shorter and shorter in different colors, until last month she shaved it all off. Can you imagine? I was horrified, but tried to just accept it. I don't care what she looks like as long as she eats… and lives."

She spoke softly and with the smooth articulation of one who has had to tell her story more than once.

"We are a good, loving family," she sputtered. Ah, yes, the inevitable need for self-defense. "Nothing like this has ever happened in our family. Her father and I have been happily married for twenty-three years and we have given our children a stable home with love and attention. I just don't understand any of this." Her shoulders dropped.

As she spoke, I tried desperately to think of something to offer her. How can I be seen as the expert here? I've been a member of this club for less than six months. I should be asking her for advice, how the system is run, what to expect through it all. Somehow I was hoping our meeting would enlighten or encourage me. Why would she think I could tell her anything? Yet she looked at me with sad eyes of solicitation. *Sweet Jesus, give me some words for this woman.*

I told her of the literature that was helping me. I told her about my love letters to Jenna and how helpful I thought they were to us both. I tried to reassure her, and myself, that this might not be all our faults. Mostly, I listened.

After an hour, we stood and hugged and both said let's do this again, yes, let's. But we never did. In fact, I never noticed her at the clinic after that.

As I walked into the teenage wing of Desert Samaritan Hospital for that evening's visit with my daughter, my mind was split with two thoughts. *Boy, I am glad my daughter isn't as bad as Carol's*, and *What if this is just our beginning?*

Chapter Seven

Ninety-One Pounds

For the next three weeks, Jenna attended Willow Creek full-time as an outpatient, which meant three supervised meals a day. As her weight went up, however, her emotional state went down, and her severe depression presented an enormous challenge for her to maintain any school life. She was losing her grip on her classwork, and finally had to drop her upper level math and science classes. Yet even as the possibility of not graduating with her class loomed, my perspective had shifted, and I could not care less about a goal that had previously seemed so important... and a given. Now, my overriding mission was to get and keep my daughter healthy and stable. Nothing else mattered. Funny, how quickly one can reshuffle the priority cards when a new hand is dealt. We were back to the ground floor of Maslow's hierarchy of human needs: Survival.

Jenna's Journal

October 12

It is so frustratingly hard. I had no idea it would be like this…but I'm glad it happened, for some twisted reason. It's just so difficult to get back, regain my parents' trust as well as my own, and to shut out my thoughts. But I have definite hope and confidence in myself. I just have to think of Germaine, my role model. But I can't start to get fully better until I leave the program. Because until I do, I am constantly under that pressure of them keeping tabs on my weight and how much I eat. All I want is to not have to think about what I eat; to just fucking enjoy it. But I have to wait and wait and wait until my mom and Tom stop questioning everything I consume.

OCTOBER 21

I had a really nice day today. Mom and I went to Fashion Square together. We got pretzels at the mall and when we came home I watched *Fried Green Tomatoes* and had some Subway sandwiches. Forgive my focus on food. Right now I am at the Coffee Plantation, all by my lonesome self and loving it. I am trying to come up with ideas for my room, which I have yet to decorate. I guess this summer I was a little preoccupied, or unmotivated and uninspired.

Lately I have been remembering things that I forgot about myself, and finding poems that I don't even recall writing. And although I haven't been writing poetry, I am still expressing myself in other creative ways. I just can't wait for the day that I start loving my body, as is, all the time.

OCTOBER 23

I feel so trapped. And hot. And full. And sad. I feel like I am dying. Why does this have to be? How come every time I start to do so well, something happens to hold me back even further?

I am so lost and scared
I can't breathe
I don't know the way.
Why can't I find my way?
I need to scream
I need to cry
I need to be alone forever
It's not stopping.
Why won't it just end already?!

How come I can't stand my friends? How come I hate it so much when people touch me in any way? How come I hate being around people so damn much? Fuck it all!

The outpatient routine put new stresses on me, too. It was a one hundred-mile-a-day travel: take her to the clinic, on to school, home, back to clinic, back home. I never resented the time or wear, particularly since I knew she was being taken care of during the day, and safe in our home at night, but I felt my own physical stamina wavering from the stress, and I knew I had to take care of myself or I'd be no good to anyone. I mustn't fall into the same trap of trying to be the perfect mother of an anorexic.

My own days at school kept my mind and body occupied, but Jenna's condition would waft in like a damp chill over me at odd moments. One day at our faculty lunch table, a colleague told a joke that ended in a punch line about an anorexic Santa. He glanced my way suddenly realizing what he had said and apologized clumsily.

"It's O.K.," I reassured him. "Really. Please don't tiptoe around me. I can take it," I said, trying to offer him and everyone at the table an understanding smile.

I was now getting calls throughout the day by Willow Creek, insurance, or outside doctors for any number of reasons. Teachers are nearly impossible to reach during the day, so phone tag took a lot of my day's energy. In the middle of lecturing on technical writing or leading class discussions on Shakespeare, I would be startled into a stun-gun reminder of my family crisis by my vibrating phone. *Is this urgent? Can I steal away from class? How is Jenna? Has something happened, or is this just another detail from our health insurance company?* My students noticed my random agitation from time to time. I always kept my private life out of my classroom, but I have learned over twenty years of teaching high school that teens can be exceptionally sensitive and supportive when a teacher is in personal need. I did not want to share details, but I did finally let them know that my daughter was seriously ill, and I was very worried about her. Without knowing any more details, they were always kind and patient with me.

Jenna's disorder had another effect on me in the classroom. My eleventh grade honors classes, in particular, were the brightest, most energetic and mature students around. These kids were motivated about learning and enthusiastic about life in general. I sometimes scanned the room, or came away from a one-on-one interaction with one of these students, and felt pangs of sadness, anger, even resentment. Sometimes I hated, for a moment, these beautiful, thriving girls. I knew I shouldn't, and would immediately scold myself, but still the feelings stopped me cold from time to time. *You look so beautiful, so clean, so healthy and balanced. My daughter was like you just a year ago. What happened and why can't she be healthy and happy like all of you, damn it?*

Here's the dirty little secret. So many of these young ladies aren't all right at all. The smartest and prettiest young ladies cleverly conceal their most serious issues—anorexia, bulimia, self-mutilation. I have witnessed it all. Planted by parents' expectations, cultivated by their own ambitions, and sown by a culture of mammoth peer pressure, these overachievers can also excel at self-abuse. And they can do it invisibly, at least for a time.

One morning, after an especially trying weekend at home with Jenna, I came in to work feeling the emotional weight of the past year all over my body, wondering how I was going to pull off another peppy "Good morning" to my students, feeling like the mime who lifts his hand from chin to brow in an artificial *It's Showtime!* grin. I sat down in our department office and tried to collect shreds of energy. In came Barbara. She and I had gone to high school together twenty-five years earlier, but didn't know each other well; now we were teaching side by side. Barbara lets you get to know her gradually, and we were becoming very good, solid friends. A strong, earthy spirit who seems to devote each day to figuring out what the matrix of life is all about, she is a mix of herbal tea and beer, incense and cigarette smoke, meditative music and rock and roll, as she chooses a warrior's path into too many daily battles on our campus, desperate to "not let those turkeys get you down." She does not lead an easy or extravagant life. She lives simply, in an existential form of communion with the world around her. Working on a teacher's salary, Barb lives modestly; there is no room for waste. So when she walked up to me in the office before school and handed me a fifty dollar gift certificate for a visit to her own massage therapist, I was overwhelmed.

"Valerie," she said softly, "you need this. Do it. Don't thank me."

I had never had a massage in my life. I fought back tears of gratitude at her thoughtfulness, and the very notion of someone taking healing hands to this worn-out body and battered mind. I couldn't wait.

I made my appointment with Patty for that Friday at four o'clock. I found my way to her tiny suite in the heart of Scottsdale's older artsy business section, nervous about this new experience, but eager to just let go. I felt fully prepared to drop my body into the skillful hands of a masseuse. Entering her small ante-room, my transformation began. Every inch of the cozy surroundings exuded peace, with dimmed lighting, soft tones of peach, mauve, sand, and creamy white, motifs of cherubic angels, flowers, and candles everywhere. Miniature bottles of scented oils for sale sat on a shelf alongside potpourri and incense sticks. This was a delightfully cluttered cubicle for the senses.

"You must be Valerie," Patty announced, as she entered from another room.

"Yes. Hello."

I suppose I was expecting the stereotypical large Swedish woman named Olga with man-hands, but Patty was not. Close to my age, a very petite, attractive blonde, who couldn't have been much taller than my five foot, one inch frame, she offered a smile and a soft hand.

She won't hurt me, I secretly sighed to myself.

For some silly reason, I felt like I had to explain why I needed a massage.

"Did Barb tell you about my situation?"

"She said your daughter is facing a life crisis," she tactfully answered.

I summarized our situation, my emotional state, and how on the edge I must be for my friend Barb to order up such an act of kindness for me. I am sure this wasn't necessary, as all day long this woman is kneading her fists into the stresses and turmoil of people's lives. Everyone has a story. Everyone needs a massage.

She led me into her massage room, which was even darker than the first, illuminated only by candles. Barely wider than the table itself, the room demanded intimacy. Patty put me at ease immediately. Something in her spirit just flowed out calm and understanding; I had stepped into a sanctuary. She explained the logistics of a massage session, offering my option of limited clothing if I desired. I chose to give in to the experience that awaited me and submerge myself in total nakedness. No place here for false modesty; I had been wearing enough masks lately.

Patty asked if I wanted a truly deep massage or a more mild one. I thought, *Hell, I don't know—this is my first.* But I was so readied by now for complete detachment from my real world, so I said, "Bring it on!" She smiled.

The only sounds came from subdued, white noise music, the kind designed for meditation, prayer, and massages. It seemed the very music of Earth, rhythmically breathing in and out, harmonizing with Nature, asking nothing in return. Almost melody-less, yet full of order. The rest of the room was silent, except for an occasional moan from me as I learned to let go. This dark little spiritual cave seemed suspended from the rest of the world.

And so our session began. Drenched in lavender oils, her expert hands mapped their way across my shoulders, back, waist, arms, palms, fingers, thighs, feet, even down to my toes. My head, neck, elbows, temples, even ears all received her loving attention. She kneaded fingertips into my calves.

She pressed palms and fists deep into the musculature of my whole frame, firm then soft, then firm. I could feel the very toxins seeping out of every pore.

I tried not to think about Jenna or any other piece of my world, aiming to be totally in the liquid moment. As issues of work or home inevitably started to sneak in, I swept them away fast and dove into the white noise around me. Patty worked slowly, methodically, patiently, and as she finished her last restorative stroke, gently whispered, "With love, from Barbara."

I wanted to cry.

My hour massage took nearly three!

This angel of mercy spent three times longer on me than was required. As it was her last appointment of the day, she could give free reign to her healing art on this most needy client; and she did! I couldn't believe so much time had passed. A more generous therapist I cannot imagine.

She smiled at me and said, "Well, you really needed it, I could tell. You are going through a lot right now. Your body is a testament to that, every inch of it. And I wanted to help in the only way I can."

Leaving me alone in the room for "as long as you need," Patty quietly closed the door behind her. So silent was my space, I could almost hear the candles drip. I prayed for time to stop. *Leave me right here, Lord. Let me stay in the comforting womb of these walls, for as soon as I leave it, I return to being the nurturer, the caregiver, the person who is supposed to have all the answers, all the healing power herself.* Alone in the candlelight I felt peace. Here there was no time, there was no struggle, there was no fear. There was no anorexia nervosa.

Patty had warned me not have any big plans afterward, and now I knew why. Remembering her caution to sit up slowly,

I felt dizzy and nauseated, as a rush of blood swept through my body. My head felt four times too big and my body felt like it didn't exist. How I drove the thirty miles home, I'll never know. I was melting Jell-O, boneless and formless. I collapsed into the sanctity of my bed and empty sleep.

As Jenna managed to keep herself out of in-house treatment, the next transition was to attend school during the morning, then drive herself to Willow Creek for the afternoon. She was now in control of most of her meals. I tried to trust this independence, but her depression seemed no better, she was losing weight again, and she was very cold all of the time. One afternoon, I got an urgent call at school from the clinic saying that Jenna was hypothermic and I needed to take her to the emergency room right away. In a panic, I rushed right over. As I pulled into the parking lot, Jenna flippantly walked out and plopped herself into the car, acting quite annoyed by what was happening.

"This is so stupid. They didn't have to call you. I'm fine, just a little cold." This was October, fall in most states, but still very warm in Arizona.

Her fingers and lips were blue, the veins in her arms prominent.

"Jenna, you're more than a little cold. Your temperature is several degrees below normal. Hypothermia can have real consequences. The people here know what they are doing."

"Well, I don't understand why they're making you come all the way from school just to take me across the street to the stupid emergency room!"

She started swinging her leg.

The hospital attendant ushered us in to a sterile emergency room bay where we sat, not saying a word. What was there to say, after all? My mind wandered back to when this all seemed to start. Feeling like a half life-time, instead of the five months it was, I was still trying to make sense of it all, of how our lives had been completely upended by this monstrous mystery. Every day was long, every night was longer.

Finally, after over an hour, an attending physician burst in, examined Jenna, and, noting her referral from Willow Creek, bluntly, with an air of accusation, asked her, "So, why don't you eat?"

Jenna just shrugged. Then he left us with, "Well, we'll run a blood culture on her and see what's up."

In our stark curtained cubicle, we spent three more hours of strained silence, with the occasional stilted conversation interjected. When the doctor finally came back in with little or nothing to report, I plaintively asked, "Then what do we do?"

Despite his being fully aware of her anorexia, his insensitivity stunned me. He looked directly at me, not his patient, and said, "Put a sweater on, I guess."

I was outraged. Here was an opportunity to put the fear in my daughter, to emphasize to her what was happening to her body and how food would help, and he blew it! Jenna looked at me as if to say, "See, I told you I was fine." This moment made me suddenly feel as if I were dancing alone. *You're all just watching me dance, even Jenna, watching me watch her starve as I dance faster and faster. But this is Jenna's song.* I felt that thick, negative energy lurking in the room with us. She had her own dance partner, all right, but it wasn't me.

After another couple of weeks at Willow Creek, Jenna had again played the game well enough to gain enough weight and be released. She was up to ninety-one pounds. Though hospital administrators still had their doubts about her stability, she had hit what they calculated to be a viable weight to warrant full independence from the program. Except for strongly recommending follow-up counseling, there was nothing more they could do, that is, unless her weight dropped. Jenna was permanently discharged from Willow Creek. We were on our own.

I wanted to believe this was a positive sign that she could handle her day-to-day structure, yet each well-intentioned day seemed to strip another pound or two from her, like layers of the self dropping away.

Within the next two months my daughter would lose another thirty pounds.

The Friday night she was discharged, Tom and I picked her up to take her home and found her in such extreme anxiety that I was already questioning the decision. I needed a quick strategy to calm her.

"I tell ya what," I offered, "Let's avoid the going-home traffic congestion, and spend some time at the mall before we hit the freeway. What do you say?" I was certain the artificial lilt in my voice was transparent.

"Sure," said Tom.

"Whatever," muttered Jenna.

As we three wandered through the busy Friday evening crowd of shoppers, Jenna's anxiety took form in her face and body. Tom and I walked on either side of her, like sentinels to her well-being. She showed no interest in anything and seemed to gaze right through the faces of fellow mallgoers.

"Ladies, let's go into Z-Gallerie. We always see cool things there," Tom suggested.

"Oh, yeah, I love that store. You do too, don't you, hon?" I asked Jenna. A shrug.

Once inside, Jenna wandered off from us. We finally found her at the end of a long aisle of art, staring at a canvas. I walked up to her and stood silent alongside. Minutes passed as neither of us spoke.

Finally, "I like this." *What? She likes.* A simple, positive three-word statement that struck like a thunderbolt. Something on this earth is pleasing to our girl.

"It is fascinating," I offered.

We were staring at a work by magic-realism painter, Michael Parkes, entitled *Swan Spirit.* Parkes's uncommon style weaves themes and images of fantastical, surreal time and space with voluptuous females and wild animals. In his *Swan Spirit*, set high up in a periwinkle-blue sky, a young girl stands above ephemeral, lilac and cream-colored clouds, balancing on thin stilts, a wide dreamcatcher sort of hoop encasing her. Gowned in white, with a white ribbon pulling back long, brown curls, she stands in trepidation, one hand on the hoop, the other supporting her chin in reflective gaze. Just beyond her in the sky, a stunning morphed figure of half-woman, half-swan floats outstretched in ballet form, back arched, head back, wing-arms extended in a posture of complete freedom and celebration of the female self. The girl is transfixed by the woman, curious, yet a bit frightened. Poised between childhood and adulthood, she seems mesmerized by the transformation that lies in front of her. Beneath her are her companions in this metaphorical journey, three swans in flight, guiding her way. Mixing themes of innocence and enlightenment, *Swan Spirit* speaks to the dangerous, yet exhilarating, threshold every girl to woman must cross at some point. *Am I ready?*

Like the girl in the painting, whom she clearly resembled, Jenna stood equally captivated by the piece. Her whole body posture seemed to say, *I must have this painting; it is me.*

I looked at her face, searching for insight. *What secrets lie in this image that clearly speak to you and for you? Can the keys to your mental prison be unlocked through this art? If I stare at it long enough, will I come to understand you better, Child?*

Even though *Swan Spirit* cost more than this teacher could afford at the time, seeing her passion for something emerge told me I had to find a way to put it in her hands. But before I could say anything, she snapped herself out of the canvas and back into the present moment and said, "Let's get out of here."

Uncomfortably silent on the ride home, breath heavy, Jenna, with all the earlier anxiety returning, kept fidgeting violently in the back. Once home, I saw fright in her eyes as she went through the motions of trying to resettle in the house.

She found me sitting in the living room and sat down beside me. Finally, her voice burst, "Mommy, I am so afraid of dying tonight!"

"What? What are you talking about?" I shot back.

She was in the eye of a full-blown panic attack.

"I don't know. I just feel like I won't live through this night. Help me, please. I can't breathe. I don't know what is happening. I just know I am going to die before tomorrow. I can't sleep. If I do, I won't wake up. Please understand this. Oh God, this feels awful!"

"Honey," I wrapped my arms firmly around her and pulled us both down onto the living room floor, "Hold onto me. Everything will be all right. You are not going to die. Do you think the hospital would have released you if they thought you were in any danger of dying?"

"I don't know. I just know how I feel. I am so, so scared. Mommy, please don't leave me."

"I won't, sweetheart. I will see that you live through the night, I promise. Listen to me. Look in my eyes, love. You are home. You are safe."

We lay clutched together on the soft carpet for hours before her breathing calmed and voice lowered. I rubbed her back and stroked her hair, telling her stories in a soothing voice to quiet her negative mind. Finally, her body stopped shaking. Eventually my heart did, too.

October gave way to November, mother gave way to daughter. Jenna had turned eighteen, and with that, I had far less authority to govern what was deemed best for her. Eighteen is such a milestone birthday. Adulthood? Not really. Emancipated? In many ways. Independent? Hardly. I bought two gifts to commemorate my daughter's eighteenth birthday: one for her, one for me. Somehow I needed to mark that I had gotten her this far and she was still alive. Funny, that never seemed to be noteworthy until the last few months of our lives together. I bought a small necklace for myself, a sort of tribute to our relationship: a teardrop topaz, her birthstone, with a tiny diamond at the tip, my birthstone. For her, *Swan Spirit*, for which she gushed her gratitude to Tom and me and promptly put in her closet. I was crushed. But even as it sat in the dark for months and months, I knew that she loved it, that it held secrets of wisdom for her, and that some day she would hang it on the wall. When that happened I would know she was going to be fine.

Without the structure of Willow Creek, we were all floundering. Jenna proclaimed newfound enlightenment on the subject of nutrition, but her eating didn't improve. She rebuked anyone for comments made, questions asked, or suggestions offered regarding her situation. We were expected to leave her the hell alone in this, thank you very much. Her leg motions became so exaggerated that, as we ran errands one evening and stopped at a bank drive-thru, our car rocked so noticeably from the swinging that I almost had to ask her to step out; this behavior was so nerve-rattling!

It was now the end of November, and Jenna looked forward to being a bridesmaid in her cousin's Thanksgiving wedding. But the leg swinging continued, and I told her that this behavior was completely unacceptable and that I could not allow her to participate in the wedding if she could not control it.

"Jenna," I told her in my firmest mother-voice, "you absolutely cannot be shaking your leg like this during Erin's wedding. We're not fooling around here. I swear to you, I will pull you out of the ceremony or festivities if this takes away from your cousin's day. You have simply got to find a way to control this!"

"I will, I will, Mom," she answered. "I promise, it will not be a problem. I will take care of it."

Yeah.

But she began to work hard at breaking this obsessive habit and, indeed, had it under control in time for the wedding. This perseverance gave me renewed hope that Jenna-Marie can do anything she decides to do, including eat.

Thanksgiving was days away. Usually my favorite holiday, full of family traditions without all the trappings of Christmas, I now found myself in dread. Thanksgiving. What is it about? Food.

Planned for my sister's house that year, the day loomed in front of me. No one knew the anxieties that rumbled in my gut. Would Jenna's disorder prove disastrous to the day? Would her progress be set back? Would she be able to eat *anything*? Would anyone make cruel comments? Would my own mother be hurt by Jenna's not eating? Would the whole day explode in my face? Thanksgiving. How do we all give thanks for the bountiful goodness in our lives? By gorging ourselves to the point of discomfort. It felt like the ultimate showdown: *"Gunfight at the Thanksgiving Corral" – An Anorexic Confronts the Ultimate Enemy: A Table Full of Relatives and Food!*

Not to shirk my familial duties, I armed myself with the resolve to maintain a sacred tradition, and with my assigned list of contributing dishes in hand, pulled out my years-old, literally battered, spiral notebook of recipe cards to prepare my shopping list. Sitting down in the early morning hours before anyone was up, sipping on a cup of hot black coffee, I began to roam through the recipe album stuffed with newspaper and magazine recipe cutouts. I ran my fingers up and down each recipe card, allowing my mind to drift back to days and foods throughout the years. Dishes I hadn't made in years. As my children had gotten older, and our lives busier, I hadn't realized what little cooking I now did. The tattered, dog-eared cards, the best recipes stained with the very ingredients written in their success, sang old songs to me:

Gram's Fantasy Fudge
Marsha's Cool Rise Coffee Cake
Sour Cream Apple Squares from Norma
Mom's Good Quiche
Nate's Boy Scout Oatmeal Scotchies
Esther's Brethren Cider

I kept thinking back to when my children were little and there was time for all this cooking, and suddenly missed these times when our family life was simple and I thought I'd be married to their dad forever. I sat in the quiet kitchen and could almost smell my memories. I thought of friends I hadn't seen in years who had so generously shared their beloved secrets for culinary ecstasy with me. I thought about the old days when Valerie had been much more domestic.

What an issue eating had become in our house of late. I had now become painfully aware of the two faces of food: how it comforts us, yet can leave us guilt-ridden, how it causes disease, yet also prevents or cures others, how it brings people together, yet separates us by culture, how it nourishes the body, but only if we have neither too little nor too much, how it is so damned important to the anorexic and the obese. I thought of my Jenna, and as I sat at the kitchen table in the early morning stillness, tears dripped down to add new stains on to old cards.

So, how did Thanksgiving go? Numbed by the fog of anxiety, I honestly don't remember, and that is the truth. I do not recall any scene, so I guess there was none. I'm sure I brought my stuffed celery, cucumber salad, and apple pie. Jenna probably helped me. Perhaps everyone there either tried not to notice Jenna's food intake, or lack thereof, or just kept silent in their stolen glances of curiosity. Maybe I avoided taking note myself of what she was or was not eating. The day came and the day went.

Two days later, my niece's wedding proved to be a challenge in new ways. It was a frigid, rainy day and Jenna's navy satin bridesmaid's gown was sleeveless with a scooped neck and back. She had her hair styled in a graceful pile upon her head, and wore elegant jewelry and three-quarter length white gloves. She looked as lovely as she could at that point, and I tried not to acknowledge to myself how gaunt she appeared. I was also afraid she would catch a cold in the bleak winter air. Jenna stood in attendance at the altar, legs still, body still. I thought, *if she can control this complusion, she can do anything.*

Following the ceremony, Nate was standing in the church's vestibule as he waited for the reception line to form, and overheard a young man make a snide remark about his sister's form. Nate was devastated. He wanted to turn to the insensitive dolt and rail against this display of ignorance. But he permitted decorum to rule the day, knowing that he or any of us might just as easily have been as thoughtless before living with an eating disorder up close. Slurs are different when arrowed toward those you love.

Jenna's Journal

December 30

> At the moment, my physical feeling is the kind I wish I could have all the time. My stomach is pleasantly full, but not the kind like after a Thanksgiving meal…more like you just had a slightly spicy soup on a cold winter's night… the perfect amount at the perfect temperature. I feel healthy, satisfied…and nourished. It's a safe feeling. I want of nothing.
>
> It's a few hours later and all I can think about is pancakes. All I can think about is how it would feel to wrap my lips around the fluffy, sweet, dry, bready stuff with the sweet, hot blueberry glaze filling my mouth with flavor. But I'm not even hungry. I just want it.

Not long after, one Friday evening, a longtime friend of mine stopped by the house with some school materials. On her way out, Lenore paused at the door with me and after asking a quick "How's Jenna doing?" began to tell me about a television documentary she had just seen on self-destructive behaviors in teen girls.

"You know, Valerie, every one of these girls is in totally destructive lifestyles, and in every case the counselors found that it all traced back to their parents' divorce," she blurted.

Hot blood rushed to my brain, and I felt my knees weaken. "What's your point, Lenore?"

"Well, maybe Jenna is just now reacting to your divorce from Jim. I know she seemed to take things real well at the time, but these issues can come back to haunt parents years later and with serious results!" Her voice now sounded like barking at me.

At this point Tom joined us at the front door and he could see me begin to tighten into a full body clench.

"Lenore," he started to intervene.

"Look," she went on, "I know the divorce was a good thing for everyone. But kids often can't see that. Jenna probably doesn't realize it herself that that's what's going on here. This show I watched focused on a girl who cuts herself. Y'know, they call them 'cutters.'"

"Yes, I know," I said quietly. "I've had a couple of students who do this."

"Yeah, well, these girls can't express their pent-up anger at their parents and lack of control in their situation. So they inflict pain on themselves to distract themselves, numb themselves, express themselves, I don't know. And the show pointed out that there's nothing parents can do about it at that point."

By now the late afternoon sun had set, and the small entryway in which we three still stood was turning dark. I felt completely trapped and couldn't seem to move, as if I were wearing cement shoes. My voice would not shift into gear to tell my friend what her words were doing to me and to ask her to leave. I stood there like a stone, just taking her well-intentioned, yet unsolicited, pummeling. I silently begged Tom to bail his wife out.

"So," my little voice finally found itself, "what you're telling me is that my daughter is now slowly starving herself and in great peril of losing her life because of something I did over eight years ago *and* there's nothing I can do about it now, and this is to make me feel better? What do you expect me to do with this information?" My voice was now getting louder and I was losing my usual stoic control, tearfully blubbering through my words.

Just then, Jenna burst through the front door and caught us up short. We froze in awkwardness. *Gee—can you tell we were talking about you?* Without saying a word, since Jenna no longer troubled herself with cordialities, she brushed between Lenore and me and bounded up the stairs to take her nightly position of Couch Fetus in the loft.

Needless to say, that pulled the plug on our discussion. Lenore gushed an apology for having made me cry and quickly made her exit. I sat on the bottom stair in leaden disconsolation. Tom stood in complete helplessness.

For days to follow, I thought and thought and thought about what Lenore had said. While Jim's and my divorce was an amicable one, any divorce has a major impact on its most innocent, the children. To this day I still occasionally offer a prayer that my children forgive me for the very act that saved my emotional life, and theirs. I could never get Jenna to say that our divorce was a bad or wrong thing. And I knew how very much she loved Tom, and shared in the happiness that he was part of our family. Yet, could Lenore be right? Could all this be because of my failed marriage? Perhaps every one of us has our own assigned demon.

alive?
It mutates you!
Now, let's obsess
WHY
Scream
Plumpity Plump!
"I'm thinking about you, but not too much."
Every minute
NO
Put up a fight
problem is deep
explode!
Hole
a selfish person
I am not who you think I am.
LESS
EAT
Body
sick
TROUBLE
WHY
INSIDE
OOPS, THERE IT GOES.
Eat Me
STOP
heartbreak
BEWARE OF EXTRA
DEMONS.
RETURN.
You put it there.
WATCH OUT FOR EXTRA
Oh, no, not another
SLIM
nagging sense of guilt.
bottled up.
NO
Trying
WHY?
stop
ALONE
Confession
pissed off
PRISONER
ADMIT IT
DO THIS "DON'T"
DON'T swallow.
Let the headgames begin...
EAT

Chapter Eight

Seventy-Five Pounds

Jenna's Journal

January 1

"I would proudly partake of your pecan pie."

Through December to March, our family moved in the bizarre rhythm of a maintaining anorexic. Jenna made it vehemently clear to me that she was responsible for her recovery and my interference in her eating would be a detriment. She was adamant that I was not to ask if she ate, whether at school or at home, or why she wasn't having certain foods. I tried to keep silent, but I made a mental note of every aberrant habit, every bite consumed and meal missed. She removed herself from any family involvement with food. She refused to eat dinner with us; she'd wait till hours after we were finished, come downstairs like a furtive mouse looking for scraps, and eat odd things. She sometimes ate a half dozen pickle spears in one sitting, then smelled like rancid brine for days. If she happened to go to the bathroom after eating, I discreetly listened for any sounds of purging. Despite all her insistence that this was not about weight or dieting, she insisted on fat-free foods and no meat. Grocery shopping together was torture; we were now on two separate planets. When we tried to walk the aisles together, she became anxious and tearful. One day we had barely entered the store when she and I stood in the produce department, each in the physical grip of distress, as she loudly spewed at me, "You just don't understand!" I was all too aware of shoppers clear across to the bakery department staring in bewildered curiosity. I didn't care.

We finally agreed to shop separately, each with our cart. It felt oddly comical as she and I would pass in the aisles and nod in mute respect. She had all her own food—tofu, veggie burgers, Pam spray, fat-free milk, Eggbeaters. It was like virtual food. I knew she had been educated at Willow Creek about nutrition, the importance of a balanced food plan, and the healthy caloric intake necessary for recovery. When I reminded her about these things, she became hostile and indignant and accused me of interfering. "I know what I'm doing. I've learned all about this stuff. You have to trust me; I have to do this my way!"

But her way was not working. She was despondent, and losing more weight. The scale behind her back read, with no emotion, "Seventy-five pounds," but all I heard in seeing it were exclamation points.

Jenna's Journal

January 2

> I'm such a terrible, horrible, no-good, very bad person, I swear to God. I lie much too much for any human being, much less a Catholic sweetheart, and one day very soon I'm sure it will catch up with me. It's just gonna run right up behind me and bite me hard in the ass. Of course I'm aware that I'm losing weight! I look in the

mirror every damn day and watch a skeleton sway and dance in front of me. It's a miracle my jeans even barely cling to my protruding hipbones. God! I'm starting to resemble the worst of those at Willow Creek. But I have a plan, dammit! It's in my damn plan. It's not my fault it had to be delayed this long. Soon I will eat regularly and I will eventually start to gain the weight back. But I can't handle it when she tells me so, and when she asks me what I plan to do about it. Talking about it just makes me not want to do it. I don't want to admit my intentions aloud. I can't.

I will get better.

I will get better.

I will get better.

I will get better.

I will get better

January 6

My problem is just that once I get the vision of the food in my head, how it looks, how it feels, the texture, the preparation of it, what it's like to bite into it, to taste it, to chew it, to swallow it… I can't get it out of my head. Right now it's a stupid bagel with cream cheese. And oh! The numbers! Even better! So what will things be like after tomorrow? Easier? Harder? More enjoyable at all, or just that much more painful?

Weekends still loomed interminably long and frightening for Jenna. The approaching inactivity of forty-eight hours of inactivity petrified her, even while at home. "How will I get through the next two days with nothing to do?" she'd ask me, her voice shaking. Yet, there was nothing she wanted to do. Friends stopped calling her or inviting her to join them. Jenna had no interest in them; they had no understanding of her. Their lives were way too normal and high school-like; hers was way too close to death. She began to try to sleep the day away, partly out of depression, I suspect, and partly to avoid one or two meals that way. I couldn't bring myself to wake her, reasoning that she could reserve more energy, demand less of her tiny, worn-out body that way. She would rise as late as one o'clock in the afternoon, with her first "meal" being an apple methodically cut into easily a hundred pieces that would take her a full hour to eat. I would see her from across a room and try to understand the supreme battle going on in her head, and the resolve it took to swallow those hundred pieces.

Afternoons were used up going to movies alone, or lying in a fetal position under an afghan, watching television upstairs in our loft. Then dinner, very late, maybe a can of soup. Was this indeed a slow suicide?

I begged Jenna to live up to her agreement with Willow Creek to find a counselor she was comfortable with, and get some worthwhile therapy, along with taking her prescribed anti-depressant medication. She knew the hospital exit drill and had each time agreed to the stipulations. But once home, she insisted that she would not see a counselor.

"Mom, I don't need to see anyone. I can handle this on my own. I don't want any medication either. I hate drugs. I don't want to get hooked on anything."

I was paralyzed by my impotence here; she was now eighteen and reminded me what little authority I had over her. The "good mother" was trying to grant her the emancipation she craved and legally owned, without allowing her to die. Enter negotiations. O.K., I browbeat her into a compromise. She promised to be faithful with her medication if I backed off on the counseling refrain. To reassure myself that she was indeed taking her pills, I set out each day's allotment on the bathroom counter, then checked later to see them gone. I tried so hard to convince myself that she was indeed being a good girl and taking her medicine. Yet I wondered why I wasn't seeing any significant improvement from her anti-depressants.

"Jenna, are you taking your medication regularly now?"

"Yes, Mother," she pounded the word with sarcasm, "I told you that I am. Get off my back about it, okay?"

"Well, frankly, I don't understand why it doesn't seem to be helping you much."

"The doctor said it takes awhile. I know what I'm doing."

"Do you really?"

"Yes. Trust me, won't you?"

"Honey, I'm trying. I really am."

One night after she assured me she had just taken her pills, I was gathering her laundry and picked up a pair of her size zero jeans. Can you imagine someone's body image who wears a zero? My hand, without any conscious connection to my brain, found itself slipping into her teeny front pocket. *Please, please don't let me find anything there I don't like.* I thought of muffin crumbs in the disposal. My fingers reached the bottom of her pocket to find not one, but six tiny pills that she had been tucking away from possible discovery. No! No! The negative voice was winning. Addiction turns people into liars. Addiction turns people to betrayal. Addiction is a desperate thief.

I cannot trust her. I cannot trust my daughter, still. What do I do now?

"What are these?" I screamed at her. "Why are these pills here? Why have you not been taking them and been lying to me about them? Why aren't you trying to help yourself? You won't take your pills, you won't go to counseling, you won't eat. How can you tell me to trust you? I don't understand any of this! Tell me what the hell is going on!"

The iciness of her stare back chilled me. "Mom, I hate drugs. I don't want to become dependent on any outside measure. Don't you get it? I need to kick this by myself." Her voice was strangely calm.

"But you're not, are you?" I lashed back.

"Well, you just have to let me do this on my own, my way."

I had become sick of this mantra. No medication, no counseling, no eating. It was becoming impossible to even fake confidence in her solo flight to recovery.

Every battle we had usually ended with me reminding her that I would rather she hate me but be emotionally and mentally well, if that's what it took. I would choose her leaving home in anger, never seeing me again, if it meant she were well. I would freely give up her love for me if it were the only ticket out of this hell for her.

Jenna's Journal

January 11

> "If you don't say something, it doesn't get said."
>
> Yes, it really, truly amazes me how completely mental I am! No, seriously. I can't believe how insane I have driven myself. How incredibly obsessed I've allowed myself to become. I drive myself mad with my thought... I'm obsessed with control... truly that's what this is all about.

The whole food and appearance aspect is just an outlet. I need control. I sit and I think and I think and I think until I'm satisfied enough and I've planned things out perfectly and I'm contented. Then it's such bliss to be content. That's why it's so, so sad when something unexpectedly goes wrong and interferes with my plan… and the control is lost.

January 15

It's just food. It's just a meal. No big deal, really. It comes and it goes and another will always follow. There will always be something to look forward to. Try to arrange your life according to time, not according to how it is in relation to the meals. It's just gonna come when it comes. Just let it go. It's okay. I'm all right. I'm all right.

I'm just gonna kick back here and relax in this body. I'm just gonna lay my skin down and do or not do what I want with it. Appearance is too totally such a singular, small part of the huge big picture! And it's so changeable! So what's the big deal?

I have lived with the mentally ill before. I grew up with a father who was manic-depressive. The term these days is *bipolar*. All I knew was that my dad was always dealing with emotional issues. He suffered numerous nervous breakdowns which led to several hospitalizations, and finally had to give up his career in newspaper work.

As a child, I never understood the complexities of mental illness. Actually, who does? But I always sensed that my childhood household wasn't normal. Gray images seep back into my consciousness even today. My father pacing back and forth in our tiny living room as he fought crippling anxiety. Daddy lying on the living room floor for hours on end, rubbing his chest and staring at the ceiling in search of answers to impossible questions. Watching a grown man sobbing at the kitchen table for reasons he could never put into words. Accompanying my mother to the hospital one night to visit him, only to be told I was underage and had to sit alone in a dark car in a pitch black parking lot for two hours until she returned. Holding the hand of my father who was temporarily rendered mute from another shock treatment. My dad waking me early on the morning after my high school graduation so that I could turn in another letter of resignation for him because he couldn't face the task. Coming home from a day of college classes seeing terror in his eyes, as he tells me in unveiled language, "I didn't think I'd make it through the day, Val. I'm glad you came home when you did." As an eight-year-old, or twelve-year-old, or sixteen-year-old, I always felt perplexed by such unhappiness, and I wondered why I wasn't more effective in reasoning him out of his despondency. Why couldn't I just make him all right? Shouldn't *I* be able to make him happy?

Although each of us will experience our moments of depression on one level or another, it remains a conundrum. Long or short-lived, it sucks the very breath of the life force. Those who have not suffered from the clutches of chronic despair find those who do easy targets for ridicule, condemnation, or dismissal. Even for loved ones of the mentally ill, it is difficult to grasp that its targets may be, or at least feel, truly helpless. "Why can't you just snap out of it," we admonish. "Just be normal, will you?" It could be that they cannot.

In the home of the emotionally ill, every family member is held hostage. Normal needs or problems must be slipped under a placemat somewhere in order to devote oneself to someone else's issues that are always bigger ones. One must never do anything that could possibly trigger a setback. I remember feeling this with my father. How my older sister, Marsha, my mother, and I always tiptoed around his feelings; he was the ill one whom we must protect, even from himself. We girls had to be the strong, stable ones, never doing anything that could make Daddy worse. How could we dare upset our father when he was so clearly tortured already? We had to be mature and well-behaved because he was a mess. It is emotional ransom. None of us knew what comment or action might possibly send him into the relapse of a breakdown. I am sure this is what formed a "good-girl syndrome" in me, and in my sister. There was simply no room in our family dynamic for Marsha and me to get into normal kid trouble.

When the family member with a mental illness is the parent, it forces a role reversal. We had to be the adults because he was often the child. We had to keep our emotions light and in check because he was prone to sob in front of us. My sister and I even had to endure his psychological and verbal abuse toward our mother for fear of how *he* would feel or what *he* might do if called to the mat on it. And when the adult could find no reason for life, the child had to find wisdom beyond her own years to offer him.

"He's sick, girls," my mother would offer in excuse. "We have to try to understand." This was an impossible task for two little girls.

As I watched my own daughter's mental derangement keep her from enjoying a stable, healthy life, I began to wonder if she had been genetically predisposed to depression through her grandfather, and if hers, too, would be a life sentence of inner demons.

Beyond my daughter, I worried for the health of my two sons during this year. I worried that their needs were being neglected, that their school year would be minimized, their own problems pushed aside. It became too easy for them to become passive, almost invisible, while Jenna was center stage, and I am ashamed to admit that I really can't tell you what was going on in their lives that year. I kept them fed, I kept them clothed and they knew that they were loved and that I would be there for them, too. I prayed they would forgive me for how much Jenna required of me, and begged God to take care of them until I could better divide my focus. They went about the business of high school and college, kept their grades up, gently wrapped their arms about me when I needed it, and avoided their sister entirely. Captives of mental illness—the loved ones.

Greg became reserved and absorbed himself in his solitary hobby of cartoon artwork, exhibiting great talent and insight. He rarely spoke of Jenna's condition. But sometimes when we sat down to dinner and she chose not to participate, he stared at her empty seat and looked sad. Or he'd sit closer to me while we watched television, and occasionally speak just above a whisper, "I'm worried about Jenna, Mom."

"I know, sweetie. I know. We're doing all we can. I think she will be O.K. She'll come out of this. We just have to give her some time to work this out."

Nate took the more combative approach, impatient for his sister to be her normal self again.

"Well, I don't get it! What the heck? Why doesn't she just eat? Why is she doing this to us? Mom, are you aware that when you're not home, she runs up and down the stairs over and over again, I guess to lose more weight? This is stupid!

Doesn't she see what this does to you especially, Mom? She's just being selfish! I just don't get it." I knew that even his anger was fueled by love and understandable frustration.

And then there was Tom. As our family drama played out, I often found myself struck by the supreme patience and devotion of my new husband. Having lived the single and peacefullly self-indulgent life of a bachelor until age forty-five, Tom certainly must have entered this state of matrimony and instant parenthood with valid concerns about adjusting to three kids and a wife under one roof, albeit a large one. Add to that the mental health challenge of a lifetime, and I wouldn't have condemned him for any urge to run away. And yet, never did he sway in his commitment to my family and me. He accepted the role of stepfather with great dignity and balance. He did not try to be Dad; they had one. He just tried to add to their lives in a positive way. The children knew that he loved and cared for each of them. Most of all, he was always there for me. He did not add to my guilt or grief, but endured my many wails of worry, holding me until my spasms of fear would subside.

Many nights I just had to get out of the house to breathe fresh, demon-free air. Tom and I would bundle up against the cold night air and walk. Living on a golf course as we do, we enjoyed the privilege of stepping out onto the ninth fairway, dark and quiet and private in its after-hours isolation. Outside, in the dark, I could breathe. Away from the dynamics within our walls, I could exhale. Oblivious to the freezing air around us, we would sit for hours on the grass or nearby golfer's bench and look back at our beautiful new home. One of us often remarked how this two-story house, lights glowing from every room, never let on to outsiders the raging fight going on within. I believed that this house was filled with love and that it *would* defeat the enemy inhabiting it temporarily. How anxious every one of us was to just get going with our blended life. I wondered, *was this to be what the rest of it looked like?* I tried to brace myself for the possibility that our girl might be at the start of a lifetime of mental illness. My bones told me we would love her through whatever would come.

In January, Jenna announced that she was beginning a Weekly Challenge, as she called it. Every Sunday, she would confront an eating disorder issue in the risky arena of the public. One Sunday afternoon, coming through the door after being gone for several hours, she greeted me with a sly smile and whispered in my ear, "I conquered Dairy Queen today!" Her grin was almost wicked in delight.

"That's great," I told her, afraid to overreact and trigger a setback. I had learned to speak in my own seven-second delay, never quite sure what were the precisely correct words to utter.

Jenna's Journal

January 16

Wow, tomorrow's the big day. I've been looking forward to it for quite some time now. But there's also a part of me that's fearing and dreading it too, of course. But that's the part of me that I'm trying to destroy. I'm wondering if I'll enjoy it. The sweet, cold cream sliding down my sore throat. The chewing of the cookie dough in my teeth. You know, I skipped an orthodontist appointment just so that there would be nothing, no chance of anything keeping me from enjoying this. That's how important this thing is to me. I'm going to do it and hey—I'm even going to do it alone. I can. Pray for me.

> I often wonder what the future holds for me… the near future as well as the distant…for all aspects of my life, of course, but namely my disorder. I can foresee myself eventually being normal and having cereal for breakfast and salads or baked potatoes for lunch and occasionally a challenging food. But I know me. And I know that "moderation" has never been a word used to describe anything I do or feel. I am passionate and intense and when I do something, I do it with all of my being… I didn't diet… I starved myself. So I'm terrified that I'll end up binging and then feel incredibly guilty about it and end up purging, or go back to starvation and then keep doing a pattern of restrict-binge-restrict-binge. I don't want to do this to my body, 'cause then she'll get so mad at me. I know she doesn't deserve it. Okay, that's it; I won't allow myself to do that. I'll be all right. I can eat healthy.

Every Sunday Jenna sunk her hooks into another Everest. Every other Sunday that challenge was to be dinner out with Mom—a challenge for us both. These proved to be ritualistic departures into the bizarre. I found my own comic relief in relaying these nights the next day at school with Barb. "My Dinners with Jenna," I called them. I dreaded these Sundays, and all I could do was hang on to my patience while with her, thank her for a lovely time when we returned home, and quietly close the bedroom door behind me to exhale as I laughed and cried in ventilation to Tom. Jenna was struggling, struggling against this ferocious demon that told her everything twisted to do at the dinner table, seeking to control her, while she tried desperately to do right while out to dinner with Mom. The result was a painfully long hour of an internal battle of wills.

"Where do you want to go?" I'd ask.

"You pick."

"All right, how 'bout Uno's?" I suggested.

"No, I don't want to go there."

"Red Lobster?'

"Do they have chicken?"

"I don't think so. Olive Garden?" I tried.

"Did that chicken salad you had there have the beans in it?"

"I don't remember."

"Then let's go to Applebee's. Yeah, Applebee's."

As I approach Applebee's to the left, Olive Garden is to the right.

"No, Mom, please, I want Olive Garden. If there's too long a wait, then Chili's."

I turn in to Olive Garden. "No," she halts, "I want to go to Chili's."

"Jenna, don't do this."

"O.K., try Olive Garden." We do. Already she is in pre-eating agitation. After a twenty minute wait, "This wait is too long... O.K. Chili's."

"No," I finally pronounced, "we are staying here." We are still in the lobby.

"What time is it?"

"Seven o'clock."

"I usually eat later. Can we sit here until it gets a little later?"

Later.

"Can we sit somewhere else? I don't like this booth."

"Sure." I find myself trying desperately to accommodate her, as I know this is so extremely hard for her; she is making every effort and I will do anything to make the evening successful for her.

"This isn't much better!" Annoyed, she moves her place setting and a dessert/drink promotion out of her way. "I'm cold. What time is it? I can't decide what to eat." Tears.

"Do you want to leave, honey?"

"No. No. What kind of place setting is this? No spoon or knife? Ma'am, may I have the rest of a place setting? Why a steak knife? I want a regular one. And this isn't even clean. I'm just used to eating later."

"It's almost seven-thirty."

"What time is it, exactly?"

"Seven-twenty-two."

"Oh, you said almost seven-thirty."

My shoulders began to drop as I stifled a sigh.

"Okay, I'll have the blackened chicken salad. What kind of dressing do you have? Oh, I can't decide. I'll have the ranch, no, the Italian, no, the bleu cheese. Do you have any fat-free? I'll have the ranch, fat-free, on the side. Diet Coke."

I smile apologetically to the waitress with an unspoken plea for forgiveness.

Strangely, once the food was put in front of her, this girl would proceed to eat every bite of her order as I watched in disbelief. She ate with total abandon, looking like a starving homeless child I had just rescued off the streets. With her dinner plate wiped clean, she'd reach for a piece of my remnant lettuce, and as her own plate gets picked up by the heroic server, she's dipping her finger into her dressing for a last taste.

I notice her fingertips are blue.

"Ooh, I'm so full." This became the routine. "I ate too much. I should have saved half for later. I am so uncomfortable; I'm so full."

"Is that good or bad?"

"It's just uncomfortable."

"Right. There's no morality in it."

Through all my *Dinners with Jenna*, every server was patient, nonjudgmental, and as accommodating as possible. I knew they could read our situation. I wanted to pull every one of them aside and explain, beg their indulgence, and thank them for helping my daughter and me survive another Challenge Sunday. I had to hope my extravagant tipping spoke for us both. One server in particular had to inform Jenna, "I'm sorry, we have no baked potato." Seeing Jenna's barely restrained agitation showing in every muscle, the server went to the back, explained somehow to the chef that there was a certain urgency in meeting this emaciated girl's need. They makeshifted a stuffed potato skin with mashed potatoes from their menu. Jenna's and my effusive gratitude was met with a nonchalance, as if this were routine for him.

During our meals, we carried on truly rich conversations once we could both relax. I tried to keep her mind occupied constantly, away from the import of the eating process. *Keep talking, keep talking. Don't think about food or the fact that you are eating it.* We talked about family, school, art, music, boys, girlfriends, religion, fashion, heaven, movies, life in general and our philosophies about it. One night she remarked, "Once a week, just for awhile, I want to forget that

I have an eating disorder. No one knows me here, no one knows..."

Letting down from the tension of these evenings, I always slept particularly well, knowing that my little baby was "stuffed... so, so full." I would almost silently talk to her food: *Now nourish, nourish, do your work, replenish, restore, hold her together for awhile more.*

Jenna's Journal

January 20

I feel good. I feel very, very good and I'm not ashamed to admit it. Just a teensy, eensy little bit sick, but that's okay. It's to be expected. I had a lovely, wonderful evening with my mom to make up for all the frustration of the preceding hours, days, weeks. The pain won't last forever. Nothing bad will happen to my body because of this night. I still have complete control. Things never, ever turn out the way you plan them. Dammit and thank God.

Okay, I didn't want to have to do this, but it looks as though I have no choice. Ladies and gentlemen, we now present an extremely cheesy, extremely necessary, and hopefully to be extremely honest self-affirmation. I can be, I must be, I am a unique, special, decent, normal and gloriously abnormal human being without this thing.

January 24

So I'm sitting here in the mall and feeling not the least bit of hunger whatsoever and yet I know that in seven minutes I will consume the red apple that's sitting in my knapsack simply because that's how I planned it and wondering when the time of my life will be when I can just eat something that I feel like having because I am hungry at that moment.

It cost me two dollars to come to the conclusion that the whole point of the Challenge is to not feel obligated to go exercise the next day. And even after I came to this conclusion I still came to the mall and climbed the same flight of stairs three times.

Sometimes I think that I could suddenly just give it up. Just like that. Just wake up one morning and go about my business as if I had never even had it. There's a big part of me that believes that that might one day happen. Maybe I'll do that.

I don't know why I wrote those words, "I am sexy!" before. I certainly don't feel it. I know I don't convey it. Maybe it was just a written wish.

When am I going to realize that I am a human being, just one human being among billions, and that no one gives a goddamn care what the hell I look like? I am not the thinnest person they've seen in their life, I am not the largest person they've seen in their life, so why even give a shit as to what they think? Just fucking chill, honey-baby!

January 28

I want to be normal, I have to be normal, I can be normal, and I will be normal! I will live without this! I don't care if I am just a regular person or boring and not special—this is not the way to be

> unique. I don't need this or want it. Eventually I will be rid. I will be rid.

In the midst of these quicksand days, I was grateful for the distraction of a thing called work. Our daily work gets us up in the morning, activates our internal programming as we shower, dress, grab our keys and drive down the road without even thinking about where we are going. It is our day's purpose. Being a teacher kept me grounded. The bell rings; I'm on! In a daily routine of five periods of fifty-five-minutes of instruction time, six-minute passing periods between classes, forty-five minutes to eat lunch, make phone calls, copy materials, and meet with students, there is little time to pause and ponder anything else. Energy is directed, and that's a good thing. A teacher's day does not allow for periods of wallowing in the self. Through waiting out a long pregnancy, or a husband out of town, or impending divorce, or financial woes, Mrs. Foster must put on that confident, positive face and get over herself. My intellect stays channeled, and every student demands my attention, becoming my child for a time. It holds one together when life outside classroom walls is unraveling.

And then there were those days when it took everything I had to make it to 3:00. One morning, before school had even started, a colleague came in to the faculty office and sauntered up to me. "How's your daughter, Val?"

None of your business, I wanted to spit. I don't like Wade. He is boorish, bombastic, and boring. Three capital offenses in my book. And I know when he asks about my daughter, it's just his way of sidling close to me. Ugh.

"Actually, she's doing better these days, Wade. Thanks for asking."

"Yea, well, just brace yourself, because you can expect this to never go away completely. She will be trapped in this for the rest of her life. Sorry, but it's true. Every time I think my Brenda is over her drug thing, it comes back. Now she's charged with credit card theft and prostitution. She's just no good, doesn't talk to me anymore, and I wash my hands of her."

"Well, Wade, that doesn't describe my relationship with my daughter, and we are all just getting through this the best we can."

"Hmm, well, I'm just saying, don't get your hopes up."

Gee, thanks, you ass. That's what I needed to hear this morning to start my day. And, by the way, I don't remember asking you! Oh, why does my real voice fail me when I need it? It's that tiptoeing again.

Later, at lunch, Nurse Florie came up to me at the faculty mailboxes. "How's your daughter doing, hon?" Nurse Florie, who doesn't have a mean cell in her body, loves all and serves all, but cloaks herself in medical doom. She'll have you in the E.R. for a hangnail.

"Oh, she's doing better, thanks."

Patting my arm, she went on. "Well, honey, don't expect too much, because people don't just snap out of this. You will be in this for years." *Allow me my hope, dammit. False or true, I don't care.*

And yet, there were those remarkable fellow teachers and staff who emerged from obscurity to touch my heart. Colleagues I barely knew stopped me in the halls to express their concern and condolences at my crisis. I was mortified and gratified at the same time. *God, I didn't want to think about this right now before third period, but oh, how thoughtful and comforting.*

My closest circle of friends happened to be my colleagues, too. Everyone knew what I was dealing with at home, but I never brought up the subject, particularly at school, unless someone asked me; I didn't want to be a drag. Space between us became cluttered with superficial chitchat. I've always hated chitchat, even the word itself; it sounds like cat food. I struggled with feeling that my friends felt uncomfortable around me and were avoiding what I was going through.

Many did, however, find a way during the school day to slip in ways of letting me know they cared. People like Nancy, who told me she prays for my daughter every morning in the shower. Bill, who sent a student of his, a recovering anorexic, to speak with me and offer hope. Billie, who every other week it seemed, slipped a funny or inspirational card in my box at school. Pam, who would tell me "Good hair day!" when it wasn't, just to make me feel worthwhile. Rhonda, who often sailed into my classroom as soon as the rush of students had left to ask, "How *are* you?" and meant it, staying as long as it took for me to answer. And, of course, there was Barb, whose children greeted me with bear-hugs me as she introduced me. "This is Valerie – the one whose daughter we pray for every night at dinner."

When the occasional question came up at school, I answered candidly, but was hampered by the confines of our work environment. I hoped my eyes would somehow convey my plea for company outside of school. *Ask me, just not here at work where it's safe for you, and I can't let down my guard. Ask me when you've taken that extra effort to call me at home, or when we're alone and I can cry on your shoulder.*

In retrospect, I believe that they were letting me take the lead, and I was not so good at that. They didn't know what to do or say. After all, there was no *Friends of Parents of Eating Disorder Victims* manual for them, either. But I was left feeling isolated, especially after one asked me outright what I needed and I told her, "Frankly, lunch, or an afternoon out," but that never happened. No one whisked me away on a Saturday morning to let me safely unload. Or just forget for awhile and shop. I interpreted that to mean that they didn't want to be confronted with it, and I couldn't blame them.

And so, a distance formed between my friends and me, and it's probably more my fault than theirs. I couldn't bring myself to make the overtures, because I didn't want to dump this on them if they weren't open to it. But that's what needed to happen. I have always had difficulty asking for help, crying in front of others, calling a friend in the middle of the night. My childhood's paradigm had constructed me never to be the vulnerable or weak one. Always have to be the strong one, me. Stubborn Irishwoman. So I stifled the voice that wanted to scream, *I'm a friend in crisis. Where are you?*

Real life is messy.

What I may have perceived as my friends' failings were my failings. We fail in reaching out to each other. In asking or answering. In saying what we feel or need. In laying open our hearts. In having those most uncomfortable conversations. How many times have I not been there for others? Am I approachable? I don't know. As an adult, I have never had that one best friend to whom I revealed my good, bad, and ugly. I have learned that adult friendships often come customized, in a sense. I shop with this one, have wine with that one, talk sex with this one, talk cooking with another, share my spirituality with one, but my politics with still another. It is no one person's job on this earth to be all for me.

Chapter Nine

Sixty-Six Pounds

On the last day in January, Tom and I enjoyed a rare Sunday out by attending The Phoenix Open golf tournament. Walking the vast hills, fairways, and desert gullies of north Scottsdale's renowned Tournament Players Championship Country Club gave us time to talk, soak up the crisp Arizona sun, and escape from our world back home for a few hours.

"Tommy, on the way home, let's stop at my folks', please? Daddy always loved the Open, and I just feel the need to share our day there with him." Tom Stapleton's world, in younger, healthier times, revolved around golf. Before his numerous nervous breakdowns had forced him out of his career as a newspaperman, he covered Phoenix's bourgeoning golf scene in the fifties and sixties, had a short stint as part owner of a golf magazine, and he never missed The Phoenix Open.

By now, it was clear to see that he was losing his tug-of-war with the mighty Alzheimer's, which he had fought for three long years. His personality and nature had changed as he became increasingly belligerent and hostile toward my mother. We had begun to worry about both their safety. This insidious disease had also robbed my dad of his greatest asset; a previously gifted intellectual and debater, he now struggled and stumbled to form the simplest words. This was his hell.

Tom and my mother and I sat around the kitchen table as I tried to help Daddy feel like he had been at this golf event, too. He stood in the right-angle crook of the kitchen cabinets, leaning against the counter for support, and could only stare at me. At moments he seemed vacant. But mostly, I could see that he was right there with us mentally. He just couldn't express it.

"And Daddy, Tiger Woods was there. He was amazing to watch. Your favorite, Phil Mickelson, finished very strong, too." My father's eyes sharpened. "We had such a great day out there." He smiled, perhaps with a memory of his own.

My mother's voice punctured the air. "Val, honey, how's Jenna doing?"

Crash.

"Oh, uh, well, not so good lately, Mom. She keeps to herself a lot and won't see a counselor." I felt my whole body deflate as my eyes worked quickly to blink back tears. It was a constant juggle to answer my mother's questions with honesty while shielding her from the grimmest details of our year.

"So, you mean, she's still not eating?"

"Well, not much, Mom."

Awkward silence oozed down the kitchen walls around us. I looked over to my dad. He tried to speak. He could not. The accelerating deterioration of his disease was taking increasing command of his speech. He stood for unbearable minutes while, out of respect, we three granted him the chance to try.

"J-J-Jenn..."

We waited. Every muscle in his face contorted in an angry, bitter grimace as he fought desperately with his brain and tongue and throat and mouth to simply say what was lodged in his heart.

"She... is... argh! Can't. Can't!" his feeble voice seethed between clenched teeth. My father's face transmitted more sadness and frustration than I had ever seen through all his warrior years on the mental health battlefied. He wanted desperately to participate in our conversation, to perhaps encourage his own daughter, or give her advice, or offer insight, or just lend sympathy.

"I know, Daddy, I know," I tried to reassure him, as if I knew precisely what he was trying to say. I doubt that I convinced him. He pounded a fist on the counter and looked away in embarrassment.

I gave my father a long embrace and said we had to get on home.

Back in the car, I said to Tom, "I am so glad we took the time to stop to see him. I think he really enjoyed hearing about The Open, don't you?"

"Yeah, babe. He can't talk much anymore, but we could read it all in his eyes, couldn't we?" he answered.

I nodded. "It was all in the eyes."

How grateful I will always be for that afternoon, because the following evening my sister called to tell me that my father had suffered a stroke. The doctors had informed my mother that given the nature of his stroke, along with his advanced Alzeimer's Disease, it was doubtful he would be coming back from this. The next day I stayed with Mom at the hospital, watching for any sign that the doctors were wrong. I finally left in the evening and couldn't face going home, so I took myself to the movies. I sat alone in the dark theatre, grateful for the anonymity and isolation, and quietly wept. I cried for my father. I cried for my daughter. I cried for my mother and myself.

My father is dying. Perhaps, if the gods must take him, they will spare my daughter. Please, I cannot lose them both.

The next morning, Jenna asked if I was making a trip to the hospital that day. “Yes. Would you like to come with me?” I asked.

“I think I would.”

I hadn’t urged any of my children to visit their grandfather yet. I suppose I kept thinking they would have time, or maybe wanted them to gauge their own comfort level in doing so. Besides, he was completely comatose and couldn’t discern who was there. I now wish I had insisted that they learn the ritual of family love in dying.

Walking into her grandpa’s room, my daughter stopped short, not prepared for the trauma of seeing him reduced to such a lifeless lump. She walked to the side of his bed, gathered up his lifeless hand and gently stroked his fingers, all while speaking small talk in hushed tones. I simply stood and watched. She took out a childlike valentine she’d made of red construction paper and taped it to his bed rail, hoping he’d somehow see it or know it was there. Next, she placed a feather-light kiss on his cheek and said goodbye. Her emotional strength was evident, and I found comfort in thinking this meant she truly had the inner weaponry to win her own battle.

Over the next thirteen days it became apparent that while my dad’s life was not in imminent threat, it was in ultimate disrepair. As he remained in a coma, doctors were now certain that he would not even regain his previous state of an agonizing decline. They suggested that the merciful thing, both for my father and my mother, was to “accelerate” the natural inevitability of his dying. *Oh God, am I hearing you doctors correctly?* In their ever-so-tactful, clinical way, they proposed that nourishment “be withheld,” using the detached passive voice preferred in these situations. They would slowly reduce my father's intravenous liquid nutrient intake. Eventually, his organs would shut down and he would die peacefully. Is there such a thing? My mother, sister, and I listened carefully to every word being laid out to us.

"How long will this take?"

"We never know, but generally a few days to a couple of weeks."

"Will he feel anything... any pain or awareness?"

"No, you can be assured of that."

Really? How? How can you be assured?

"Is this legal?" my mother asked.

A slight smile. "Oh, yes, of course. It really is the compassionate thing to do." The alternative was to maintain him in a vegetative state for an obscenely indefinite period.

My mother's pleading eyes looked to us to help her come to a resolution. While such a decision was excruciating for us all, my sister rose to what the moment required, and came to a place of merciful comprehension. With great tenderness, she held Mom's hand and told her that it is her decision, but that this was probably right; it would be okay. Despite feeling numb, I knew it was best for our mother, and she had to be our greatest concern now. Then my voice spoke for me, saying in a soft voice what I knew she desperately needed to hear.

"Mom, you need to trust the doctors. It will be fine. It's what we should do."

But it still lay at my loving mother's feet in making the agonizing decision to leave her signature above the line reading, "Wife."

We walked away with papers signed and I felt nauseous. What had we just done? Was it the right thing? Would he know? Would he forgive us? Would God?

I prayed it would all be over soon.

That night I stayed up late, grateful for the house to finally be asleep. I curled myself into a fetal ball in my overstuffed, navy velvet-sculpted chair. Its big, round, tufted arms seemed to hug my body in sympathy. Motionless, I tried to let the stillness of the deep night suck the day's toxins right out of my pores as my mind worked to sort out the conundrum in front of me. My daughter continues to deny herself sustenance, while I find myself drawn into imparting the same onto my father. We all knew, without doubt, that he would have agreed with the decision. My father was ready. The two were not parallels, yet I was struck by the cruel irony of the gods.

Why does everything seem to revolve around blessed FOOD?

Our next step was for my sister and me to help Mom make some difficult decisions, including arranging for Daddy's funeral. It seemed so bizarre to do this while he was still living. Two days after the beginning of the end, the three women in my father's life sat in the quiet, sickeningly sweet-fragranced conference room of a funeral home, with its traditional dark wood furniture and silk plants, and sifted through pages of choices in announcements, prayers, flower arrangements, music.

Next, we strolled most uncomfortably through casket displays. My sister and I worked to convince my mother that she needn't go into debt in providing her husband with a decent, even lovely casket, and together we finally settled on a handsome copper bed. Going through all the motions of this behind-the-scene ritual of passing a loved one on, with the atmosphere of death all around me, tiny needles of thought kept stabbing at my brain. I kept pushing them away, but knew what they tried to say.

The next morning, Marsha, Mom, and I met for breakfast with plans of going over to see Daddy afterward. Sitting in the restaurant's cozy alcove decorated in cheery yellow and blue country motif, we ladies enjoyed a much needed hour of coffee and conversation. We felt a strange sense of peace and comfort in each other's company as Mom took her daughters through her usual interrogation method of finding out about her grandchildren. She embraced the most mundane details of our children's lives, with the loving interest only a grandmother can have. We kept the talk light, each of us desperate for a sense of routine life, albeit a false one. Eventually, however, we came around to questioning our decision to withhold nourishment from Daddy, even as we ourselves enjoyed a sunny breakfast in downtown Scottsdale. Each lady rotated reassurance to the other in a sort of circular pact; we knew our dad and we knew he would tell us this had to be.

I dreaded the end of this familial breakfast, aware of the anguishing visit that awaited us. None of us sensed that as we sat over eggs, bacon, and bagels, in a nearby hospice my father left this world.

As we were leaving the restaurant, something compelled my sister to decide she should visit my dad later when she would have more time. It seemed illogical to me that she would change plans so abruptly, and she didn't really offer a specific reason, but we agreed to take her back to Mom's house to get her car. While there, my mother noticed the blinking phone message from the hospice telling us to call immediately.

"Yes, this is Loretta Stapleton. Oh, I see. Uh-huh. Oh, really, oh my. Yes, we'll be right there," she said, while sending hand signals to Marsha and me of a mock throat slash, or perhaps a thumbs down, that clearly communicated *Daddy died*. What a strange way to be informed.

Arriving at the hospice minutes later, it was completely shocking for us to walk in to my father's room to see him lying there, alone. No one in attendance, no one to escort us in. It struck me that had we not stopped back home unexpectedly, and received the phone message, my mother and I would have casually walked in on this scene minutes later completely unprepared. My sister's last minute decision had providentially spared us this.

Then I thought, if we had perhaps skipped breakfast, or not had that refill of coffee, or just planned an earlier visit, might we have been present at his hour of death? For a moment I felt guilty knowing that his wife and daughters were laughing and chatting and embracing even as he died. But then again, perhaps that was right.

We spent the rest of the day finalizing arrangements with the funeral home and our priest. I finally got home late in the afternoon, completely spent, emotionally and physically, collapsing in Tom's arms. This dear man began to slow dance with me in the middle of our wood-floored kitchen. In a slow-as-molasses two-step to silent music, he held me in the rhythm of love, caressed my grief, letting me know in his quiet, manly way that everything would be all right.

Alzheimer's Disease takes its sweet time in draining the life out of its host. It kills brain cells gradually in a sadistic tug-of-war with Time. My father's stroke was just that, a stroke of God's hand in sparing, not just Thomas, but all who loved him, the indignities and suffering of interminable deterioration. His few years of living with this ailment were mercifully short, compared with so many others. Alzheimer's Disease ended his life; a stroke ended his Alzheimer's.

The day after my father died, I resolved to keep a Sunday date I had made earlier with Jenna to go shopping for a hat for each of us; we both love hats and I was encouraged to see her wanting to do anything. It was Valentine's Day, and while in the mall, we were greeted by a handsome young man handing out pink or white carnations to every lady. I tried hard to enjoy the day with my girl, to pretend my world wasn't unraveling around me. We stopped in one of Jenna's favorite shops where she saw a bare little slip of a party dress that she wanted to try on. The very request was odd since she had hidden herself in piles of shapeless clothes for all these months. Was she secretly looking ahead to regaining a social life that included parties? I answered with a ready, "Okay, honey," but inside I cringed because I knew she would look dreadful in it. *Don't show your body*, I thought, *the more we see, the worse you look*. In retrospect, I now believe that, subconsciously or not, she wanted me to see the degree of her illness.

She called me in to the dressing room. As I entered the tiny space and shut the door behind me, I looked up to stare at the sight in the mirror. A figure I didn't recognize was staring back at me with a feeble grin. My daughter. I had not seen her out of her baggy jeans and threadbare sweatshirt for months, and I wouldn't have known her on the street. All that came to my mind was that I was staring at the victim of a concentration camp, one who was near death from starvation. Her disjointed, misshapen form was marked with bony, angular protrusions everywhere. Skin the color of gray paste covering flat, stick-like arms like a wire hanger frame. Lifeless eyes peering from within dark circles. She stood there, knees knocking, shoulders stooped, looking like a warped, broken dolly. This was the child entrusted to me. I could not even fake a normal response this time.

I stood stunned for a moment. Legs like sand, heart tripping over itself, I passed out. Right there, in the confines of this miniscule dressing room, I collapsed against the door.

"Mom? Mommy! Are you O.K.? What's wrong? Talk to me, please!"

I began to recover my physical senses, yet could not budge from the floor in the corner of the dressing room. The stress of the year, the grief of the week, had finally drained me of all reserves.

"Look at yourself," I could only whisper. "You *must* see what is happening!"

"I know I'm too thin," was her pat response in monotone.

I shook my head. "You have no idea... you just don't get it."

We left the store, she empty-handed, me empty-hearted, silence between us; our shopping day was over. I walked aimlessly through the mall as we somehow made our way back to the car. I heard, saw, felt, knew absolutely nothing. I cannot remember a more surreal time of almost floating through space from shock. I could speak not a word.

On the way home, I railed to deaf ears about her need to see a counselor. I insisted on a weight update. It had been some time since I had known her weight, and this journey we were taking was so fraught with the unknown, the blurred, and dark. A number on a scale would either validate my concerns, thus arming me, or alleviate them somewhat. A number is tangible. Jenna agreed, but I had long ago removed our scale at home. So we stopped at my high school and walked in to the nurse's office.

"Hi, Florie. My daughter and I just want to use your scale. Is that all right?" I worked to keep my voice normal-sounding.

"Sure, hon." Nurse Florie flashed me a look of alarm as she glanced at my daughter. I was becoming accustomed to that reaction.

Because Jenna and I respected and followed her therapists' edict to never allow the sufferer to know her weight, she kept her back to the scale's display. In the darkened examination room of a high school nurse's office, I froze to the floor, now staring back at a scale that read sixty-four pounds. *Sixty-four pounds.* I blinked in disbelief, and tried to stifle my breathless panic. Jenna had lost more than half her body weight. And body weight means more than fat; it means muscle, bone, organs, hair, brain cells. *My God.*

Mother's Journal Entry

I'm fighting again. The strains, tears, anxieties, fears, agitations of combat are back. Take action, Valerie, take action. What to do? I don't know! Do something today! But what - who - where? She is down, down in weight, I can't even write it, lest she find this, but the number is burned in my brain. She is cold. Her fingers are bluish. "Hang on, baby, hang on, till I think of something. Mommy's coming."

despair, despair
I am in total
despair, despair
despair, anger,
fear, fear, fear and loathing
despair
Please, please don't
let me lose her.

Please, please, please
Lord, heal my girl.

My father's funeral was the setting for new strains, as family members and friends, whom we hadn't seen in a long time, gathered. Jenna looked particularly gaunt in a long, straight, shapeless, colorless outfit, a gunny sack of a look. These days she repelled physical touch from anyone but me, and as guests arrived and drew up their own sense of etiquette to give her the obligatory hug, I watched her stiffen and recoil. Throughout the day, I could almost feel the silent stares of those who hadn't seen my child for some time. I knew they must have been shocked, despite being aware of our situation. An anorexic has her own look. It is not that of a thin person, a fashion model, a drug addict, or one with cancer. Even AIDS has its own distinctions. There is just something about anorexia that defines it. Perhaps it is the way the facial muscles are all but gone, with the skin so tightly pulled across cheekbones and chin, transparent as wet tissue paper, making the eyes almost bulge. The teeth look too big and ears protrude. Maybe it is the dry, thinning hair or the prominent blue veins, or the elderly hunch on a young person's frame. Could be the lackluster eyes and vacant stare.

I had become used to people's glances and murmurs; that didn't bother me. But this day was for my father, and I resented any distractions from our paying respect to him and his life. Today was for Thomas Stapleton.

Daddy's usual clean-shaven, crewcut look had given way in the last few months to a transformation. As his days living with Alzheimer's Disease lengthened, he had watched his mobility and independence wane and didn't get to the barber as often, and his head of thick silver hair was now long and combed back. His increasingly hostile behavior and awkwardness in fine movements meant he could no longer be allowed around a razor, so for the first time in his life, had grown a beard. In variegated grays and silvers and whites, it too was thick, shaped nicely into a dignified v. He looked like a handsome, venerable sea captain. I pretended, as I looked at him in death, that that was what he was, instead of an old, tired newspaper man with too many demons of his own. We couldn't bear to dress Daddy for the afterlife in a stiff, artificial suit; he didn't own one and had always opted for a Southwestern bola tie when formality was required. Marsha and I convinced Mom to bury him in a favorite navy blue Pebble Beach golf sweatshirt. Old salty Tom had finally found comfort.

Finding my own proper moment to kneel before my father's casket to pay my final public respects, my memory rewound back to my very first funeral as a child. I was about eight years old and being led into a small, unfamiliar chapel where my great-grandmother, we called her Ma, lay in waiting, of a sort. Some adult relative took my hand and ushered me to the open casket and single kneeler set up, then left me there! I didn't want to go up close, but they made me. *Hey, I'm not ready for this physical proximity with death; I'm only eight, for Christ's sake!* I felt a mix of fear and confusion and resentment at having to play grownup with no instructions. I didn't want to look at Ma, didn't want to, didn't want to, but, of course, did. My first dead person. She didn't look much like I remembered her. She had been made up in garish, saturated makeup that made her look like a careless clown. Lipstick too dark, rouge too red, powder too pale. *Don't stare too long. Don't take too long. People are watching and waiting for their turn. She sure is old. And smells funny. Maybe it's the sickeningly sweet odor of this cold heavy spray of roses on her box. What am I supposed to do now? What do I say? Do I talk to her? A prayer maybe? Well, God, take good care of Ma. She always told long funny stories over and over and over again, and pinched and squeaky-kissed my cheek with a "God love ya!" with every visit we made to her stuffy old apartment in Paterson. And she always had little wrapped candy in a curly milk-glass candy dish. I liked her and knew she loved Marsha and me. Bye, Ma. O.K., how was that? Can I go now?*

But I felt a strange comfort in kneeling at my father's coffin. I bid him final, long-sought peace and begged that he intervene with the angels on behalf of our Jenna. *Look over her now, Daddy. Please save her. Please be powerful in your new translation. Please surround my daughter with a powerful shield of healing and security. Save her. Rescue her from the clutches of this evil force. Make it go away. Now.*

A member of our family brought me to my lowest point that day. As I returned to sit in the front pew just a few feet from the open casket, she sat down with me and began grilling me on what I was doing about my daughter's condition. "Val," she said, "she looks like death warmed over!" My face flushed. I wanted to scream, "No, my *father* looks like death warmed over. As a matter of fact, he is!"

At that moment, I felt the room swirl around me. Sitting in the front pew as Daddy's service proceeded, my mind kept wandering. *Don't think, don't think, don't think about death, don't think about her. Don't think about funerals. Focus, Focus on your father. He deserves that. Live, Jenna. For God's sake, live.*

As friends and family stood at the gravesite, I bid farewell to my father by reciting a favorite poem, "Crossing the Bar," written by Alfred, Lord Tennyson when in his eighties and near death. "… And may there be no moaning of the bar when I put out to sea... I hope to see my Pilot face to face, when I have crossed the bar." I wanted to stride over to my daughter and in front of all who love her shout, "There is peace when someone aged seventy-four dies. There is no peace when someone aged eighteen dies!"

We returned home from the funeral and I sought solace in my favorite overstuffed blue chair. When you sit in a single chair, you're left alone. No one can cozy up next to you with unwanted strokes or hand-holding. Nobody can pull your head down to rest on his shoulder or her lap. You just get to be left the hell alone, surrounded in dark blue velvet. A single chair says to others, "Grant me some solitude." So I sat and I sat. I tried to sort out the puzzle of life and death, and again wondered, would God take my little girl, too? That I could not bear.

The afternoon following my father's funeral, a family friend came by with an entire gourmet meal she had expertly made, as only she can. Everything from salad to dessert and even a bottle of wine. People know what to do when someone dies; they just don't know what to do when someone's daughter is slowly killing herself.

Jenna and I had been about to go out to a movie that afternoon, and although we had plenty of time, Jenna walked into the room as we were visiting, and became demonstrably rude to Susan, saying that we had to leave for the movie. Susan hadn't seen Jenna in all these months and she tried to be polite and act as if nothing in her appearance, or our lives, were amiss. But as soon as I tried to reassure Jenna that we had plenty of time, she huffed away. Sue's face went ashen.

"Oh my God, Valerie. She looks awful. Oh, I can't believe that's Jenna. I had no idea. I just had no idea."

I tried to tell you, I wanted to cry. *In fact, I've been telling you for months that she is not eating, is seriously ill, is in and out of hospitalization, and that I am coming apart. What did you expect her to look like? Now you see some manifestation of what I've been going through and why I need for you to call me and be my friend up close.* Instead, I smiled meekly.

Jenna's Journal

February 2

I wish I were still child-like.

"Bobbing for Apples"

Reach
Far into me
Eyes closed.
Swish and swirl around
Trust that you'll
Find something.
Through the cold and wet and dark
Find the treasure
Bite down hard
Hold it tight
So that you'll never
Lose it again.
Taste
Enjoy
Pulpy sweetness.

February 9

Yeh! I just thought of a new challenge food to try, but get this—it's really a challenge meal! I am going to combine two foods that are each difficult for me but that aren't difficult alone to make an entire meal out of it. Oh, I am so excited. It will either be the teriyaki chicken with an original cookie or a Subway sandwich with an original cookie. Maybe some other time I'll have a Blimpie with a candy bar or cookie or something. Yes! I'm so pathetic. Actually, on second thought, maybe I wouldn't have the teriyaki chicken with a cookie—it's enough on its own…but maybe one of those grilled chicken salads or something. Oh yes. Lord, help me.

FEBRUARY 17

My List of Foods I Have Faced and Conquered

~~Choc. chip cookie dough-raw~~

~~Olive Garden Shrimp Alfredo~~

~~Snickers~~

~~Fruit pie~~

~~PayDay~~

~~Butterfinger~~

~~Sbarro's slice of cheese pizza~~

~~Blueberry muffin~~

~~Pretzlemaker – garlic~~

~~Bacon burger-Applebee's or Chili's~~

~~Mozzarella sticks~~

~~Chicken Caesar salad~~

~~Hawaiian chicken~~

~~Coldstone Creamery~~

~~Gardetto's red~~

~~Gardetto's purple~~

~~Snyder's Hanover~~

~~Wendy's fresh stuffed pita~~

~~Popcorn at the movies~~

~~See's chocolates~~

~~Kyoto Bowl~~

~~Pancakes at 5 & Diner~~

~~Veggie burger Denny's~~

~~Chick-fil-a~~

~~Cinnabon mocha drink~~

~~Higley Hot Dog~~

~~Red Lobster~~

~~KrispyKreme donuts~~

"Mommy, could we lie together?"

My little girl's deep depression was exacting its toll on every member of our family. She had become cold and mean-spirited to her brothers, distant to her stepfather and completely alien to her own father. With me, she became emotionally leech-like. So many evenings, she asked to lie with me in my bed. Dropping whatever I was doing, I would climb up on Tom's and my bed and welcome her in. I'd wrap my arms around her little chicken-bone arms as we curled together like spoons. I often felt awkward as I tried to hold her tiny, crooked, brittle body without breaking it. She just held on tightly as we talked in hushed tones about life and this mysterious *thing* that had come, we hoped not to stay. Both of us vacillated between extremes of hopelessness and faith. She, in her depressed state, questioned the meaning of life itself, and mourned the loss of her spirit and love of life. Then, nearly in the same breath, she would assure me that she was some day going to be over this disorder.

"Mom, I am not going to die. Everything will be O.K."

I wanted to cry out, "Then if you are so sure you will be fine in the future, why can't you make it be now?"

We seemed to swing in the pendulum of extremes. When I was in despair, she'd be full of hope. When she sunk down in the darkest of hours, I wove a vision of faith in tomorrow and delight in her very existence. Some moments I spoke of the magnificent beauty of life itself, a banquet put before her, and all that I looked forward to sharing with her in the future. Then, I sometimes found myself losing my grip, collapsing in a puddle of mush, crying to her that I couldn't bear to lose her. I knew she wasn't choosing illness to hurt me, and wouldn't suddenly be well just to help me, yet there were moments I pulled out the stops and begged her to do it for me. Frankly, I didn't care what the tactic if it worked. But I also knew I had to be stronger than her and stronger than any threat. Guilting or shaming her way out of this wasn't a workable strategy. Instead, I tried to let the love flow. I would love her out of this.

"I will not abandon you, love. I am here for you and will never leave you. We will see this through together." Then the quiet came.

She never wanted to leave my bed, and while I cherished those intimate moments of holding her, stroking her, being mother, I would always reach a moment when I absolutely needed her to leave. I felt suffocated by the very intimacy of it. The demon was in bed with us and I had to get away from it. There wasn't room for all three of us. I could feel it breathing on us, pulling all the walls in closer in a stranglehold. It drained every emotional cell in me. Jenna would finally, in pained reluctance, pull her little body from the temporary peace of my arms and down comforter and go to bed.

I always felt a pang of guilt. And a sigh of relief.

Jenna's Journal

February 15

I didn't want to
slip out of the safety
and comfort of
my mother's warm arms
My hair was damp
with exhausted tears
and matted against
the side of my face
as I pulled away.
My unused joints had
become stiff,
so the more
I moved away,
The more pain
and relief
I felt.
Her angelic cheek
was so soft
like a light powder
on a flower petal
as I kissed her goodnight.
I didn't want to.

Can I really do it? What makes me think I can do this? Can I? Will it be too hard? Can I do it? Can I? How can I? God, help me, please. Please! Can I? I'm scared. I'm scared. I'm scared. I'm scared. I'm so scared.

My fear lay in losing her. But my sorrow came from *her* fear. Such paralyzing, agonizing, gripping fear of life, the unknown, the future. Around my children, I had always tried to speak and act out of faith, optimism, and a love of life, and from the time she was born, Jenna effortlessly mirrored that. In fact, I often felt I had gained just as much from her; she was the truly wise child of the universe. Even as a newborn she was all sweetness and light. Born on her due date in the middle of the afternoon, she just seemed to walk this earth to bring joy to all around her.

Jenna was my baby girl who collected My Little Ponies, loved to make oatmeal cookies with Grandma, and danced for hours on end to *Disney's Greatest Hits*. My daily devotion was to be a mom who nurtured her self-esteem, empowered her to make decisions, gave her a home of unconditional love, and a tremendous belief in the spirit both within and around. "Despair is an insult to God," I'd once heard. Fear felt like an insult and a mystery to *me*, and at times I felt angry at her for seeming to reject all that I had tried to instill. *How dare you undo my work.*

We parents often see our children as little sculptures we design and mold to present to the world. They are not. We might indeed take our artist's tools to these lumps of clay and leave our marks, but once in the kiln of life's experiences, each piece undergoes its own baptismal firing of the soul. I couldn't really know what my daughter was going through, and I had to let go of my personal investment of ego. What mattered was her survival, of both her physical existence and her spirit.

Jenna's Journal

February 22

Oh, God—golly. I feel so sick…still. After crashing in early last night in a fetal position, I slept all night and woke up feeling no different than when I went to bed. I will never do that again, I can assure you.

I truly believe that if I could just get away, just start over fresh and new somewhere, I could get over this. Because it would be like I could just pretend I never had it. But I can't do that now or here. It has to be away from these people who know too much and ask too much. Is that delusional?

February 24

Wrapping your icy, burning fingers
Around my throat, you
Slowly scrape and scratch
And dig your sharp yellow nails
Into my vein
And drain
It…
Robbing me, sucking it dry,
Making me an empty one,
Void of all real life,
Joy, happiness, satisfaction, equilibrium, passion, energy, balance
Can't escape your sweaty palms
Filling me instead
With the inky black
Pollution of obsession,
Ambivalence
And panicked insomnia.

Please…
Where is the release from this
fanatic's embrace?

My daughter's existence was shrinking. Having made it through another day of school, she would come home and collapse in her negative space on the sofa. Once there, she seemed to wish life away. I began to worry that her starvation would prevent her from thinking her way clearly out of this deteriorating cycle. Some nights, after she had finally gone to bed and I still lay awake with the pangs of a caretaker's anxiety, I would slip into her room to reassure myself that she had not died in the night. Standing in her doorway, I often first gave a start that she didn't seem to be in her bed. Then I noticed, yes, she's there; there just isn't much to her. Her linens seemed completely flat. She lay there like a tiny heap of bedding. So many nights I stared down at my little girl who had stolen peace for a time at night. *Are you breathing, little one? Are you having happy dreams? Will you wake up in the morning? Will you be better tomorrow? Will I know what to do if you are not?*

I offered Jenna-pie a gift massage from Patti. She agreed. I called Patti, explained the situation, silently entreating her to not break this fragile body I was handing to her. I hoped that perhaps Jenna would come to love and respect her body at the touch of Patti's healing hands. It brought me such a feeling of peace to picture someone gently, lovingly touching my daughter's entire body with care. *Let it happen, Jenna; let it work.*

Jenna's Journal

March 1

I am a girl. I am a woman. I am a lady. I am stubborn. I am fierce. I am intense. I love jazz. I enjoy Shirley Temples with the cherry. I eat ice cream in soupy form. I mix chop suey with the potatoes so they turn orange. I have a button nose, I am flat-chested. I have wide, flat hips but a small waist. I am bothered by skinny movie stars and models. I have dreams and goal. I have an intense fear of waking up with the realization that I'm not doing what I need and want to be doing. I have great faith in the belief that God will do what's best for me and everything will work out the way it's supposed to. I am petite, small-boned. I like strawberry cupcakes with confetti frosting. Dark, deep red is my color. I will always need my mother, my mom, my mommy, mum. I cry at very few movies, but the words of my mom can make me buckle within the blink of a tear-filled eye. I know that there is no contentment like that of lying next to my mother, smelling her smell, feeling her arms safely around me. I can never have too many shoes, as long as nobody has an identical pair to any of mine. I want to step forward and forward and forward. Winter is never long enough for me. I am all cheekbones.

Days turned into weeks with no progress, and I began looking into another possible residential facility for Jenna, and kept being referred to Remuda Ranch. Located a couple of hours from our home, their program approached healing from a spiritual, Christian-based outlook. I read through their compelling materials and wondered how we could possibly pay their staggering fees if our insurance wouldn't. Could we sell our new house? Plunge into more debt with a loan? Ask friends or family for help? Beg?

Chapter Ten

Sixty-Four Pounds

"Valerie," my mother gently suggested one day, as we sat in her kitchen and she saw the effect of the last year on my face, "maybe you need to see someone."

"Huh? What do you mean?" I sat staring into my coffee.

"I think you should talk to someone—a counselor. Get some advice on how to deal with this. I'm worried about you because you are trying to take care of everybody, but I think you need to talk to a professional about all this."

"Mom, I am handling this the best I can."

"I know you are, sweetie. But maybe others can help you 'handle it' a little easier. And wouldn't it just do you good to put this in someone else's lap for a bit?"

"Oh, maybe. I don't know. I don't know anything these days." I robotically stirred my coffee, my eyes blurring with the salt of tears. Setting my spoon down, I looked up into the eyes of my mother. "I go through the motions every day in class as if I know it all, while my life is falling apart. Mom, I am in such a strange state of mind."

"That's why I think you should talk to someone who can help you better than any of us can. Do this for yourself," she said, and then added, "Do this for Jenna."

"I'll think about it," I finally offered.

After thinking about it for a couple of days, I decided that if I couldn't get Jenna to accept counseling, I'd model one who can. Maybe it would seem less threatening for her to do the same. I made an appointment to see a counselor through my school district's health plan. First six visits are free. Cool.

"May I be assigned a counselor who specializes in eating disorders?" I could almost hear chuckling on the other side of the phone. Specialize? This is free, you know. *O.K. I'll take whomever.*

Sitting nervously in the waiting room, I thought: *Run, run away now while you can. You can't talk to some stranger about all this. This is too personal. This is too painful. Run!*

"Mrs. Foster?"

"Yes?"

"Hi, I'm Tracie." All of twenty-four years old, I estimated, twenty-five on the outside. Hmm. A slim, attractive redhead, Tracie smiled and extended her hand, no doubt reading the fear and skepticism on my face. "Come on in."

Rats, too late to run now. Well, I can get through one session.

Her tiny office with the west window was bright, colorful, and way too perky, like her. Her walls a stark clinical white, she had dressed up every corner with overused phrases designed to inspire, small, stuffed animals and basic "counselor" bric-a-brac. *O.K., now Valerie, give the kid a chance.*

As I attempted to succinctly summarize my last eight months, and try to help her know my daughter of eighteen years in a few minutes, I seemed to detach from my body. I actually saw myself sitting there, *blah-blah-blah*, rambling on as she took careful notes, as I wondered, *Will she think I'm hiding some ugly family secret? Will she blame me, the mother?* She smiled sympathetically now and then, her face so young, so virginal. How can this nubile young professional begin to understand this mother? Her formally-educated mind cannot fathom the depths of love and fear a mother can know.

She looked pretty thin herself. *I wonder if she has any food issues*, I thought, sizing her up. *Geez, Valerie, get a grip.*

It took me nearly our entire hour's appointment, which actually sped by, just to lay out my situation, and I thought, *Well, now that I have invested an hour in sharing my life with you, I need to come back for all your brilliant answers to my dilemma*. But when I spoke, I left Tracie with, "Tell me how to be a good mother of an anorexic."

"Can you come back next Wednesday?" *Probably needs to check her textbooks.*

"Sure, what the hell."

That's how they get ya.

So there I was next Wednesday after work. *O.K., I'll give Miss Tracie one more session to enact a dramatic breakthrough.* I wondered if I was there for guidance in how to help my daughter beat anorexia, or there to learn how to simply live effectively and indefinitely with it. The first was unreasonable; the second terrified me.

As it turned out, Miz Tracie, ink still drying on her Master's in Psychology diploma, was the one to offer the most sound advice I heard through this long, dark ordeal.

"Valerie, Jenna is the one with the problem. This is her journey, and while you can stand alongside, you cannot walk alongside. You are wearing yourself out doing all the dancing. Has any of it worked? Only Jenna, who is, after all, a young adult of eighteen, can work her way through this. You share your daughter's striving for perfection and now you are trying to be the perfect mother of an anorexic; that is a dangerous title to take on. You cannot allow her condition to threaten your work as a teacher, your relationship with Tom, or your parenting of Nathan and Greg. Most importantly, you must protect yourself. Your relationship with yourself needs nurturing. You are beating yourself up emotionally, and that leaves you in no shape for anyone else."

"But how, how do I just live with this?"

"I don't suggest you back away from taking measures to help your daughter. But you have to carve out time for you. Don't be afraid to get away for the weekend, for example. You and Tom ought to live as normal a life as you can. Have friends over, go on a vacation, cook whatever meals you want. Allow Jenna to see normality. You and your daughter clearly have a close, loving relationship; it doesn't sound like she is doing this eating issue thing to target you. So don't allow yourself to be more victimized than you deserve. Take care of the Self."

It all sounded too simplistic to me. The scary part was that I could almost hear her unspoken words: *... because she's likely to have this disorder for a very, very long time....*

As she spoke I kept thinking, "But this doesn't help cure Jenna," and I realized that was an unfair expectation. I was the patient in this setting. Tracie's job was to counsel me, not Jenna. And this young professional was doing a fine job, as it turned out. And although I initially dismissed this somewhat "quick fix," she had planted seeds for when the time would be more right for me to follow.

On an early evening in March, Jenna boldly announced that she wanted to attend Northern Arizona University in Flagstaff the following fall. My heart sank. First, at the rate she was going, she could be dead before then. Second, there was no guarantee that my former honor student would now have the credits to graduate with her class in two months.

Then the thought of her leaving home, and my watchful eye, stirred new anxiety in me.

"Oh. Well, that's fine, honey. What made you decide that?" I dutifully responded, grateful for the mimicry of a normal conversation with a high school senior. I looked into her face, skin now colorless and stretched across cheekbones.

"Well, you know, Erin is up there with her own apartment, so I would have family there, even if just a cousin. And I really like the small town feeling there, and the pines and all...." She paused for a long, thick moment. "Plus, I think getting away would be good for me."

"Oh."

"Don't you?"

"It's so cold in Flagstaff, hon. You haven't lived through a winter there; it's not like down here in the valley. And you're always blue with cold lately. How will you do with that?"

"I'll get the right clothes. And I'll adjust. I'll be fine, you know?"

Eighteen. She's eighteen, I thought to myself. Not a damn thing I can do if she chose to leave. *You cannot leave until you are well*, I wanted to plead, but knew I mustn't.

"Well, let's look into tuition, housing, and admission requirements. Your priority right now is to pass your classes and graduate in May. We have lots of time to decide." *Why are we talking about everything except Mr. Invader standing over there in the corner, having quite the chuckle at his invisibility?* He began to take the shape of an elephant.

"I already called Erin and told her what I want to do. She invited me up for Spring Break to visit and see if I like the campus."

"How will you get there?"

"I'll take the bus. It's only twenty bucks. I can leave from the terminal in Mesa."

"Sounds like you've already planned this out."

"Yeah, well, I really have to get out of this house for awhile over the break. I just need this. It's not you; it's just the walls themselves."

"Honey, don't you like this house?"

"No, it's fine. Really, it's nice, Mom. But it doesn't feel like home. I feel no attachment to itexcept as the place where I've been sick."

"I understand, sweetie. I do. I'll help you plan your visit up north. Let's check out your warm clothes."

Half of me was encouraged that Jenna was expressing an interest in anything in the future, a sense of goals, of moving from high school to college, of establishing some independence. But my other half was not prepared for that movement to be away from where I could watch, help, intervene if necessary. Had I been suffocating her? Must I face her leaving home, adjusting to college and trying to recover from anorexia all from a distance?

Jenna's Journal

March 8

I can't believe I'm actually letting this happen to me. This is the third week in a row I've done it! I can't believe I am 1) turning into what I most fear, 2) using food as a way of dealing with my emotions, 3) letting myself and my eating habits get out of control, 4) enjoying it as I do it and yet also going crazy (literally) with guilt! I am actually at this moment considering ordering mozzarella sticks at dinner. This wouldn't ordinarily be a problem except for the fact that I am not doing things in moderation like I planned would be healthy, because I also today had about a billion and one chocolate chip cookies. Not moderations! Dammit, what's wrong with me? How did I let this happen to me? Me, of all people! I know one day everything will be okay… right? One day I will do things normally and in moderation and things will be okay. Deep breath, in and out, sigh. It hurts. It hurts.

It hurts. It hurts. It hurts Mommy. It hurts. It hurts. It hurts. It hurts.

Early March brought The Great Intervention that wasn't. My cousin, Eileen, was visiting from New Jersey, and Marsha and I met her for lunch and an afternoon of carefree girl-wandering through blocks and blocks of arts and crafts at the Tempe Arts Festival. I looked forward to a much-needed distraction from my home situation. Instead, the inevitable direction of our lunchtime conversation soon centered on that very thing. I was the captive listener as they sat on either side of me ping-ponging an unending barrage of "advice," a bite of my lunch now lodged in my throat. Questions, doubts, concerns, "I would have... You must... Can't you... Why doesn't... Why haven't you... but you needn't answer to us." I began to feel numb all over and finally sat with head bowed over my deep dish pizza, watching the melted cheese coagulate.

Marsha said finally, "Let's go. Let's all just go right now together and confront Jenna, get her to go in for St. Luke's Intake Evaluation."

I was still as a stone. *Go away, please, subject; please just go away.*

"Valerie? Are you all right? Really, Valerie, let's all three of us talk to Jenna right now! Yes, let's go! Is she home?" Their voices tripped over each other.

"But what about our day here?" I said, in the whine of a ten-year-old. "We were so looking forward to this."

"But, Valerie, this is more important, and you are not in this alone."

I was now sobbing into my iced tea. I held back from admitting my selfish, desperate need for this lovely day away from my home life. *I* needed a day at the fair! Don't you understand that? Sensing I suddenly had no say anyway, I answered with a weak, "All right. Let's go." We made our way through the crowded sidewalk booths of paintings, crafts, food, music, and performers to our car. Deadened, I was in the blur of a Fellini-like setting with the surreal sights, sounds, and colors of the festival as a backdrop to my humiliating and grotesque situation.

We came home and ambushed Jenna and her apple at the kitchen table. It was her first meal of the day at two p.m. She justifiably felt threatened, and reacted by flashing such a look of loathing toward my sister; Linda Blair in *The Exorcist* came to mind. Then, just as quickly, she agreed to leave with us in an hour, right after the apple. I sensed a strange air of relief from her.

I called St. Luke›s.

"Oh—we don't treat anorexia. I don't know why anyone would have told you that. You can take her to the emergency room or Urgent Care."

We've done that, been there.

We had nowhere to turn. We were now months out of Willow Creek, months without any counseling or medication or Ensure™ or weighing or professional supervision. We were left standing in the great cul-de-sac of options, immobilized by a wave of complete hopelessness and inefficiency.

The great intervention evaporated before our eyes. Moments earlier, we had been buoyed by the sense that something was going to be done, and it'd be in others' hands to do. Now, suddenly, all dressed up and nowhere to go. Eileen and Marsha left quickly in embarassment. I dropped onto my bed and fell into a deep sleep. Jenna went to a movie.

Jenna's Journal

March 15

I can do this. I have the power to be strong and successful in any endeavor I attempt. I remember the first time, with Dairy Queen at 6:00 and it was enough, and this will be enough. I can have self-control. I am not like Ruthie; I don't need a lock on the fridge door. I can make it. On my own. Here I go.

Okay, I am hanging on a very thin balance here. I am full. I am not at all hungry. I want to eat. I am sad. I am lost. I am lonely. I am confused. I'd like some crackers. I want some donuts. I feel guilty about the brownies. I don't want to repeat the last three weeks. I really want Raisin Bran. I can't decide. I can't decide. I have the option. Do I want to go? That's the thing, though. I have complete control…but that means complete responsibility, too. I've been so good today. Should I do it? Will

> I feel guilty afterward? Will I turn it into a binge? I can't repeat the last three weeks, not this week.
>
> Okay, here's the plan: I have to do something, so, to prevent insanity, I am going to the grocery store and I am going to buy exactly and anything I want. I have to do it. And I have to try to not feel guilty. That's the hard part. Okay. I can do it. God help me.
>
> I made it. It wasn't perfect, but it was a hell of a lot better than the past few weeks. And I didn't go to bed or wake up in such agonizing pain. I was satisfied.

The next day Tom and I had planned a much-needed afternoon out, nothing special, maybe a game of golf, just being out together away from everything in the house. But Jenna was going through a dark, dark afternoon and I could feel the long fingers of the monster grabbing hold of my throat as I spoke to my husband.

"I just can't leave her right now. Don't you understand?"

"I understand that she dictates this family!"

"Well, maybe she just needs to for awhile," I snapped.

"And do you think that's really good for us, or for her?" His ice-blue eyes welled with tears of frustration.

"I don't know, I do not know. I just know I couldn't enjoy myself out with you, worrying about her. Geeze, I love you both. What can I do?" Every muscle in my neck tightened.

"Honey, we need and deserve a little time out for ourselves. She'll be fine. Let her work some of this through herself. You are my wife, I am your husband, and the strength of our new family rests in large part on our own solidarity."

"Mom," Jenna called from the upstairs, "Can you come sit with me?"

"Tommy, let me just sit with her for awhile. Then you and I can go out later, or tonight, or maybe we could catch an early movie after school tomorrow. O.K.?"

"Yea. Sure." His eyes hardened and he turned away. "I'll be at the driving range."

Several hours later Tom came home to find me sitting out on the upstairs deck, in a deep, sullen mood.

In the soft tones of love, he spoke. "Honey, you are enabling Jenna. She knows she's calling the shots and it isn't helping her or you. I am so tired of seeing her on that damn sofa every minute she's home. Maybe I would like to enjoy that new room, too. She occupies the space, the television, and won't have a meaningful conversation with anyone - except you, of course. I love her as my daughter and I miss her old self. But it kills me to see you so beat down by all of this. You have got to be tough about some of these behaviors."

"Great," I lashed back. "My counselor tells me I am doing too much, trying all these tricks and strategies, because I cannot fix this. My sister urges me to do more. 'Valerie,' she says, 'you've got to do something; I'd hate for us to lose her,' as if I'm sitting still, passively watching my daughter destroy herself. My friend informs me I did this to her years ago and can do nothing now. You, my husband, tell me that what I am doing is wrong; I'm allowing myself to listen to a disturbed girl and thereby enable her. Too much, too little, too late, all the wrong, not enough of the right. I ask Jenna, 'What should I do for you? What should *you* do for you?' I pray for guidance. I feel nothing but confusion - blind, paralyzing confusion. Exactly what is my role? I was given the awesome privilege of mothering this child. I cannot fail!"

"Look, honey, I didn't mean to..."

"I know you didn't. You're afraid to say the wrong thing to me, I'm afraid to say the wrong thing to Jenna. Every one of us is just stumbling around in the dark without a map. But I am losing it, damn it! I have to get the hell away from her, away from here, away from everything." Without even feeling my lips move, my next words stumbled out. " So, when she heads north to Flagstaff tomorrow, I'll be heading in the other direction. I'm going to Tucson for a few days."

It was not that my nerves were shattered, as the saying goes. Glass shatters. Sharp, brittle, punctured glass shatters. My nerves were strong and thick, like tough sinews of rope. But the edges were fraying, fiber by fiber, thread by thread, uneven and jagged, with an occasional ugly and sudden tear that rips to the bone.

The next morning, Tom and I drove Jenna to the bus station. She insisted on carrying her Willow Creek-battered red plaid duffel bag herself. Looking as if the bag weighed more than she did, she slung it over her shoulder with noticeable effort and slowly walked up to the counter to pay for her ticket. I stayed at a distance, as a way of demonstrating my so-called confidence in her independence. Watching her from across the room, I thought how aged she looked, like an old woman in a young body, or a young woman in an old body. Something just wasn't right. Her spine bent over, hair long, thinned and dry, she was dressed in her same uniform of worn, raggy, baggy, formless clothes; my eighteen-year-old daughter looked so tired. Above all, she appeared weak. I worried about her being away for even a few days. I worried she would love the charming campus of Northern Arizona University and opt to leave for there in the fall. I worried she'd ride that Greyhound bus on into the horizon and I wouldn't see her again.

Tom gave her a long hug, his eyes sad, and helped her onto the bus.

"Deliver our girl safely, now," he directed the bus driver. Jenna looked back at us with a half-smile and fearful doe eyes.

Jenna's Journal

March 17

Happy St. Paddy's Day, all. I'm writing from a bus station in Phoenix waiting for the next bus to Flagstaff. I am all by myself and I am so excited. I can't believe my mom actually let me do this. All I knew was that there was no way I could spend the entire Spring Break week at home.

I'm just a bit cold. And my backpack is, like, ungodly heavy. But I need the trip to save my sanity. And I am incredibly grateful, beyond belief, that my mommy recognized that. I am so glad I made it the other night. I really believe I can avoid slipping into a bad situation here. I was very, very careful and I tried really hard to listen to myself and my body and what I needed or wanted, anyway. And because I took it so slow and was so careful, I felt more in control. And that's the key; I now have a lot more faith that I can turn this thing around. I don't have to go down that road.

I am having kind of quite a difficult time deciding whether or not to have something here. I could have an orange, an apple, a banana, or a frozen lemon Popsicle. I could just wait till I get home to have an apple, where I can take the time to actually cut it with a real knife. Plus, it's safe at home. So I

> could just wait about another hour and a half or so, maybe longer, and just curb my hunger with the remainder of my flavored water. Another benefit of this choice is that my parents would see me eating a little more…not that appearances matter. On the other hand, yes, I'm feeling really kinda sick, so I could just eat a banana or the lemon bar or try to eat the apple with a plastic knife here. But I honestly can't decide on what I want to eat, okay, now I've decided I definitely want the apple, largely because I am too cold to have the lemon bar. So…do I just go for it and have it here, or wait? Eeeehhhh….

Within minutes of arriving home from the bus station, I turned right around with my own overnight case in hand; I couldn't leave fast enough.

"Tommy, don't worry about either of us. I'll be fine and so will Jenna. I'll call you when I get to Tucson."

"Valerie, I love you very much. You know that, don't you?"

"Of course. I love you, too."

Sonoran House lies tucked back in the desert outskirts of urban Tucson, some six miles of dirt road off Highway I-10. Just when you think there can't be anything out there, that you must have missed a turn somewhere, its adobe casitas rise from the mountain landscape and draw you in.

"Mrs. Foster, welcome to Sonoran House. Please accept this warm moist towel to soothe away a dusty ride."

"Oh, thank you. It feels heavenly."

"Dinner will be served in our main dining room between the hours of five and eight p.m. Joseph will escort you to your room. If there is anything you need, please do not hesitate to call the front desk.We hope you have a pleasant stay with us."

My body was already beginning to let down.

My little casita lay at the end of a small row of other adobe suites in rich shades of earthen terra-cotta. With built-in shutters of mesquite strips on the windows, Native American art on the walls, and decor in hues of a Tucson sunset, my room was a far cry from home and exactly the change I needed. For several moments I just stood in the room. Quiet. Still. Most of all, alone, finally alone with my thoughts, in control of my surroundings, bunkered from all who could disturb me. I did not quite know how to handle the freedom. Then I remembered that my purpose in being there was to let go. Free-fall for a couple of days. It did not matter how I spent my time; no one was watching. Or needing. Heaven. I lay down on the center of the firm queen bed, closed my eyes, and exhaled.

After a long nap, I propped up my pillows, lit the sage green candle I had bought on the way, and practiced the therapeutic art of journaling. I wrote and wrote and wrote, letting my pen in hand glide without reservation across my notebook. Most important to my refuge was that for the next couple of days I answered to no one. *What do I feel like doing most at this exact moment?* was my overriding question. It felt odd, even awkward, at first. Moms don't get to think like that. Complete silence roared around me. But it was incredibly wonderful. And peacemaking. I let hour drift into hour, allowing my body to simply stop moving. I took walks along the resort, swam in the heated pool, hiked the tourist trail through the property, and listened to strains of a Spanish guitarist on the patio in the evenings, as I watched hawks glide overhead so slowly with almost no wing action, lightly catching the air currents that they know so well.

And oh, how I slept and slept, with the deep abandonment of the innocent. Most of all, I let the gift of silence and solitude envelope me. I thought about home and didn't think about home.

During the day, the desert, which can seem deceptively barren to an untrained visitor, offered a feast of wildlife and plant variety. A covey of quail, whose babies looked like fur balls on wheels, scurried across blacktop as if they knew they were not supposed to be there. Lizards, some fat and brown and gray, some sage-green-striped, and some yellow-speckled with long skinny tails curled up over their heads like scorpions, performed tiny push-ups to claim their territory. The occasional road runner lived up to his name, boldly running across the roads of the resort.

With meticulously manicured resort grounds contrasting next to the primitive beauty of raw desert surroundings beyond, the land reminded me that in nature, all is in order. Despite having lived in the desert my entire life, I was seeing its rugged beauty as if for the first time, from thorny mesquite trees, palm trees, acacia, bougainvillea with its magenta tissue-paper petals, pink and white oleander, to the twisted cirrus that resembled architecture gone awry. With skeletal ocotillo, yucca, creosote that smells like urine, cholla, silver agave, sentinel saguaros with bright red blossoms, spring in the desert delivers with brilliant magenta, burnt orange or violet. Nature was restoring me.

And to the lucky participant who rises with the dawn goes the secret sensory treat of a desert sunrise. Each morning I awoke early by some natural sense, finding early-day peace in the welcome of a chaise lounge on my tiny private patio. Just before dawn crests over the mountain skyline, one can trace the curves and angles of the mountain range in the distance and wonder just where the sun will break. Along the sparse layer of steel-gray clouds, a speck of pink tinges one tiny bit of sky foam, whispering, "Here is where I am. Right here between this cloud and this mountain is where, if you watch closely, I will soon emerge and rise." The speck turns to gold and widens, then to a glittery white as the fire star itself finally peaks. Look while you can, because as soon as he makes his arrival, you can look no more, and another scorching day in the desert is on its way.

During the dinner hour, as occupying half of a table for two, I didn't feel the least bit uncomfortable being alone. In fact, I was enjoying the luxury of indulging myself in whatever moment to moment need or sense arrived. I suspect I might have even been envied by other diners in the room. Parents of three at the next table, who struggled to mold their antsy children into mini-adults for this resort setting, looked haggard and in need of the solitude I was enjoying. I could pretend, for a time, that I had no children, no responsibilities, no ties. But in truth, I had three beautiful, precious children who had my heart wrapped around their very souls, and were I to lose any one of them, I could never recover. So I offered a glancing smile toward this young family as if to say, "I know what it's like. But cherish these moments, too."

Each night after savoring dinner I could enjoy without interruption, I strolled around the resort, stopping now and then to breathe in the sights and sounds of the evening desert. Starting at twilight and on into the night, nocturnal birds flew excitedly overhead, catching flying insects near the patio lights. Doves flying close enough to catch the light of the lampposts illuminating their underbellies darted here and there, back and forth and around in circles and figure-eights in a sort of midnight synchronized ballet drill. Those flying higher captured just enough light to look like slow-moving shooting stars.

On the third morning of my retreat, I awoke and thought, *All right, God, I give this to you to heal. Alleviate this mother.*

I strolled out to the pool one more time for a morning sunbathe. Grateful for only a half dozen others poolside, I slipped on to a chaise lounge, opened a book I pretended to read behind sunglasses, and instructed my mind to go white-blank, if it could. The March air was already responding to spring, and my body basked in the delicious mixture of cool morning breeze and warming temperatures. I drank in the sounds around me: muffled conversations of nearby guests, the sporadic splash of swimmers, and always the mourning doves. As the late morning's sun rose high overhead, I could feel my body bake. Sweat rolled down the inside of my knees and arms, waking me out of a stupor. I slipped into the cool water, almost hearing the sizzle of extinguished hot skin. Ah, relief. I swam a few laps, then was suddenly jolted back to the realization that I had to check out in an hour.

I returned to my room, my own little Shangri-La, packed quickly, and with reluctance tugging at me, checked out. Feeling rested and calmed as I got behind the wheel, I revved the engine and told myself the world was new.

But very soon a sense of anxiety crept under my skin as I looked at Sonoran House in my rearview mirror and began the ninety-minute drive home, wishing I had the selfishness and courage, or cowardice, to keep driving to who-knows-where, to never return home, at least not until everyone there had solved all of this. *What would happen? What would they all do if Mom just didn't choose to come home within an hour of when she told them she would? What would happen at school? Would my students survive just fine with a substitute? Would I get fired or be pitied because my much-deserved nervous breakdown had finally come? Who could blame me, really, for running away? I had been such a good girl all my life, never moving outside anyone's expectations (O.K., there was that divorce...). Wouldn't everyone just shake their heads in sympathy, give a tsk-tsk and move on to the next headline? But that still left Tom and Greg and Nate. And Jenna. Better go home.*

Chapter Eleven

Grace

What does it feel like to have a child die? To have the fruit of one's womb leave the world into which you brought it? To lose most shamefully at that Roulette wheel?

When Jenna was four years old, she almost drowned. I had taken Greg and her next door to visit with our neighbor, Cheryl, and enjoy her pool, as was our frequent routine in the summer. Jenna sat on the steps playing in the water, while Cheryl and I stood in the pool not more than two feet away, soaking issues and gossip in cool water. I constantly looked over to Jenna out of a mother's habit. She knew she couldn't swim, and always stayed on the steps. At one point, I glanced Jenna's way to see her floating lifelessly, completely underwater, arms stretched upward. My daughter was no more than a foot away from me and drowning!

I had only to reach an arm's length to grab her out of the water. I yanked her onto the pool deck, flipped her over, slapping her back. After several seconds which moved in painfully slow motion, she gasped on the side until soon she was crying hard and we knew she'd be O.K. Though I tried to soothe her and soften the trauma, I was totally shaken inside, as was Cheryl. Of course, I was wracked with guilt that this could happen right under my nose.

That night we lay together on my bed in the dark, watching television. She needed my comfort because she couldn't sleep; I needed her near me to know she was O.K. After a long silence, while never mentioning the day's event, my little girl suddenly whispered, "Mommy, does God ever put His arms around you?"

I felt a chill. "I think He did for you today, Jenna. He saved you, sweet." I also told her that sometimes when one dies, it's God calling you to hold you in His arms forever.

Then she started talking about what had happened at Cheryl's. My little daughter seemed to need to talk about it. She told me how she'd kept trying to call to me underwater, but I couldn't hear her. This crushed my heart like a stone.

"When I die, will I feel it?" This from a four year-old. "Will God know? Will they bury me? Will my spirit go through my eyes? Then do we start all over again as babies?" Questions spilled from her lips. Momma's job here was to reassure, especially with the long dark hours of night upon us both.

She looked at me with such tired and serious eyes, a look that seemed to transcend childhood, as if she'd just learned some great big secret. She had.

Finally, we went back to holding each other as we slept the night away together, but an amorphous pall coated my mind for days to come as I kept her just a bit closer by my side. We both had been jolted into a realization of her mortality. This beautiful, small creature who graces the earth will some day die. This made me sadder than the thought of my own death. There can be no greater sorrow than to live beyond your child, to know her dying. It must bring to the parent a feeling of failure; *Have I given you life only to have you finally die?* The irony of the universe is, *yes*.

Ah, but while you live, you will bring joy and laughter and beauty to this world. You, my child, will shine, whether for five years or ninety-five.

Now as I felt Jenna slipping away from me from her self-induced starvation, it felt like I, myself, was drowning. As if my body were weighted down with concrete blocks that read *Ignorance, Ineffectiveness, Despair.* That I was screaming for her underwater and she couldn't hear me. That my voice was lost and I was sinking steadily lower into the abyss.

Jenna's Journal

March 20

> It is Friday and I have all the best of intentions for Sunday's Challenge. I decided that if I can't start getting this under control, I'm going to have to stop challenging myself for a while until I can. Because it's not worth it. And it's killing me. I'm too sad. I am just too damn sad. And I'm lonely. And I'm sometimes weak. And I'm confused. And I'm extremely lost. And I'm waiting. Time has been so slow in passing lately. I can't stand the way my mother looks at me and all the things I think she must be thinking.
>
> Wrapped in my own loneliness
> and the blustery wind
> I shield my eyes
> with the
> dull gray overcast
> hovering above
> I huddle, trapped in my
> un-changings

When all I want
is change.

"Hello, Father John. This is Valerie." I finally turned to my dear friend. "I wonder if I could talk to you sometime about some things that are going on in our family."

"Sure, well, right now I am very busy with all the Easter preparations. How about I call you in a few weeks when things have calmed down?"

"Of course. That's fine." Click.

Why can't I reveal how vulnerable and weak I am, how in distress I am, how desperately I need others? Why can't I ditch niceties and say, "No, this can't wait. I need help! I need you to pray for my daughter!"

Jenna's Journal

April 4

Oh, I feel sooo full. It's about 4:25 p.m. It's also Easter, and I spent all of last night worrying about family gatherings and what to do about my "challenge." I didn't decide anything by 4:20 a.m., when I finally fell asleep, and didn't make a decision until I came downstairs this morning to find Miss Henrietta Heffelflopper waiting just for me in my Easter basket (somehow Mom always manages to find my favorite chocolate bunny), and instantly I knew I had to make it an all-day affair. I have been eating with family all day. I feel pretty sick—like a binge, so I have to be so careful. I already know I'll be eating, like, nothing tomorrow, but, hell, I really don't care anymore. I don't do this family thing very often and I know I'll make up for it in days to come.

April 12

Break free,
Little one…
unfold your tight little fists
release your grasp
and let go…
Fly
leap out the window
into the night
into the darkness
into the freedom
and fly free.

April 13

Things are getting scary here. Tonight, in a moment of unhappiness, I started to want to binge. Then I started to choose between bingeing and not eating at all. How did I let so much emotion get attached to my eating habits? Why do I have to wait so long to switch it off?

After giving one of my love letters to Jenna one night, consisting of a long list of the many things I loved about her, I actually found myself overpowered by the sticky sweetness of the positive mind. I had an urge to vent the counterpoints to each of these, just to keep myself sane. So I wrote it in my journal, for none to see, especially my daughter.

Jenna, this is what you don't know:

- *I am repulsed looking at your arms and feeling your exaggerated veins run up and down your flat hands and arms.*
- *I go to gently pat your bottom and feel a hard little lump in your jeans, then realize that is your bottom.*
- *In a dark setting, like a theatre or riding in the car at night, sometimes I glance at you sitting next to me and can barely see you—you're almost not there!*
- *I sometimes feel suffocated.*
- *I am incredibly sad you'll not be going to prom.*
- *I stare at your healthy face looking back at me from a photo on my desk at school and I talk to my old Jenna, begging you to come back. Come back.*
- *You are difficult to hug. I shudder when I feel your ribs through your back.*

My April birthday was approaching. By now I felt like a hank of wet terry cloth most of the time, heavy and soaked. Joys in life seemed so far away. I found my thoughts drifting to my paternal grandmother, the only one I ever knew. Even though I grew up in Arizona, far from her home in New Jersey, our family's occasional summer road trips to the East Coast served to cement a kindred bond between us. I adored her. Gram was a feisty, fun-loving Irish gal who never let family-raising, limited means, or a sedentary husband sentence her to a life devoid of fun. On any given day, waving to her husband, she would walk out of her suburban New Jersey home and board a bus or train for a day trip with her "lady friends." They'd take off for Philadelphia, Boston, New York City, or hit landmarks and monuments like Arlington or West Point, or spectacular botanical gardens throughout the state. My gram was always out to have a fine time, never failing to remember to buy commemorative spoons for her two granddaughters in Arizona to add to our collection and remind us she was always thinking of us. She had a rare joie de vivre that left a deep impression on me, though I didn't realize it at the time. I still had to go through twenty-odd years of obligatory education, marriage and child-rearing.

She left me with a lasting image of her as a seventy-three year old matriarch who, dying of breast cancer, still insisted on the family having an evening of great food, dancing, and honky-tonk music at a local Jersey pub when Marsha and I had come out for a summer visit just months before her death. The Silver Fox was a wood-paneled, loud, smoky family establishment where everyone was treated like a good friend. Typical Irish pub hospitality. We all sat at one very long table, about thirteen of us. I was sixteen, and way too inhibited for my own good. My parents never spent evenings like this, and I was awkward, yet drawn in by the very unpredictability of the environment.

As Gram's favorite piano player pounded out her request of "My Wild Irish Rose," she leaned down the long row of aunts, uncles, and cousins to catch my eye. I looked back at her. Her face was lit up with the moment, her twinkling gray eyes dancing their clear message to me, "This is the best of life, Valerie. Grab it! Enjoy it!" At that moment, her image at the table plopped into my consciousness like a little Irish elfin reminder to put on my finest clothes and attend the Party of Life.

Now, as I struggled to find any moment of pleasure in my long days, I thought about Gram. What would she tell me?

She'd say, "Young lady, you've got a birthday coming up. Celebrate it. Be with friends. Take the moment; it's all we have. And don't wait for someone to do it for you."

I told myself that I must still have a life. If I let the demon that lurks in my home strangle every last bit of normalcy from *my* life, it has won. So I planned a ladies' night out - cocktails at a nearby jazz club, then on to see Paula Poundstone in comic concert. Nine friends joined me in getting away from the day's pulls and tugs. We laughed till we cried, we gossiped, we told tales on our students, we drank, we bitched, we hugged when the evening was over. No one mentioned my current crisis, blessedly; they must have all made a pact beforehand. There was no room in our evening for sorrow. The comfort of friends was restorative. Gram's spirit floated in the air.

The week following turned out to be the proverbial reaching-bottom-before-you-can-come-up series of events. Jenna was under tremendous stress during this week. She was one of three senior drama students chosen to direct plays to be performed later that week in her high school's annual One-Act Plays. This was a traditional honor that she had looked forward to through three years in drama class, and she was not about to relinquish the opportunity, despite any health challenges.

I had never seen her this weak. By now, she required twenty-minute showers to work up enough physical strength to start her day, and was barely able to carry her backpack to her car every morning and afternoon. I fully expected her to collapse at any time. I had no idea how she maintained such a demanding extracurricular activity of long daily rehearsals in her condition. Any time not spent at school, any energy not expended on rehearsal, was spent curled in her usual ball on the sofa as she fought to maintain function.

"Jenna, are you sure you're up to this?" I asked, knowing how futile my very suggestion was.

"'The play's the thing,'" she smiled, quoting Shakespeare.

"Isn't your health the thing?"

"Mom, this is all I've had to look forward to all year. Even longer than that. My crew depends on me. I can't let them down."

Throughout this whole winter's ordeal, I worried about the seasonal flus and colds going around. Remarkably, despite total lack of nutrition, my daughter had never caught a single common virus or infection. But now, in the midst of this heightened stress, Jenna became sick with some sort of stomach flu, or so I thought. She had been working so hard, and now two days before the performance, she was violently ill and couldn't stop throwing up. She blamed it on her eating too much fast food.

With not being able to keep any food or drink down, it looked like she had dropped more weight overnight, if that was possible. I wondered how her weakened body could sustain this depletion. *How far can she go? How can this body keep existing?* While anorexics can die slowly, they can also suddenly succumb to heart failure or dehydration.

In urgency, I called my regular doctor's office for an immediate appointment and was brusqly told by a perky high school receptionist that we'd have to wait three weeks to be seen.

I don't think so. NOW!

"O.K., this afternoon? Thank you."

I felt stupid as I drove my daughter to the doctor's office. I must have looked positively idiotic, as if in an ordinary visit to a doctor he will tell us what is wrong and what needs to be done. I know what's wrong and what needs to happen; she needs to eat and she'll be all better! I also knew by now that it was just not that simple.

As Jenna and I sat in the waiting room for two hours, I was struck by the irony that for most of that time, the only other patient waiting to be seen was a gentleman who was grossly obese, easily weighing over four hundred pounds. From the corner of my eye, I discreetly looked at the two of them, trying to figure out this perplexing relationship we each have with that which sustains us: food. Some are addicted to eating it. Some are addicted to not. It is not a habit to break, like smoking, drugs, booze, or gambling, because you cannot give it up. Every single day, each of us must make a hundred food decisions. Breakfast or not? Butter on the toast? Whole milk or 2%? Bring a lunch to work? Out to lunch with friends or grab a candy bar from the vending machine? Buffet at work—chicken fried steak and mashed potatoes with funny colored gravy, or greasy soup, or less-than-inspiring salad? Or just skip lunch entirely? Regular or diet soda? What size portions in the Serve Yourself line? Mid-afternoon snack? Granola bar or Snickers? Drinks with colleagues after work? Gee - that's fattening. Cook dinner tonight? Leftovers? Fast food? Dinner out? Want an appetizer with that? Did you all save room for dessert tonight? Any left-over pie in the fridge, dear? Good God, we'd better make peace with the process.

Jenna was weighed, her back to the scale as always. Her weight hovered at sixty-four pounds, but at least she hadn't lost more. Imagine finding comfort in this pathetic fact. I sat in the cold, stark examining room listening to my doctor drone on and on in a factoid list on anorexia, telling Jenna nothing new. "...possible internal damage, decreased immunities, must eat...."

Yeah.

But at least he was trying.

Jenna looked bored.

Then something deep inside of my brain snapped in to place. I felt like I was a detached observer, watching this entire scene from a distance, and my mind was hit with a thunderbolt. In the flash of thought that can take a nano-second, but is packed with thousands of wordless meanings, I seemed to wake up. The last ten months flew in front of me and I saw myself running here and there, spinning the plates, making the calls, going through the motions. Right then I had to confess the fact to myself that that these gestures of mine through all this long year, including this latest visit to another doctor, were just that, gestures, pieces of evidence I could pile up in my defense later as a "good mother" if I needed it. If it didn't work, nobody could say I didn't try. Maybe I just wanted to cover my own ass. *Your Honor, I did everything I could; it's not my fault.* What an obscenely selfish thought.

We left the doctor's office after Jenna had made clear her usual apathy over still another scare sermon from a doctor. Walking to our car, my thoughts were reeling as I realized the futility of all my efforts. I was the one making appointments, doing research, consulting professionals, even taking antidepressants for the first time in my life. Still dancing, but the music wasn't being played for me. This was Jenna's show.

I felt utterly spent. Then a great letting-go washed over me in a strange mix of both fear and relief.

It was time to stop.

Sitting in our car in the parking lot, I turned to face my daughter and spoke with a measured firmness before turning on the ignition to drive home.

"Jenna, maybe you're not ready to be well. Maybe this just is not the time yet for you being over this and nothing, nothing I, or anyone, can do or say will change that. If you were ready, you would be doing every single thing possible. You have always stubbornly declared that you want to do this your way in your own time, and you're right. You are responsible for your recovery. I can no longer keep taking the aggressive role here. You're not alone in this. I am here if you need me. I always will be here to catch you. I love you wholeheartedly. But maybe you just aren't ready to be well. Let me know when you are."

As I drove us home, she sat silent, looking dumbstruck. When I pulled into the garage and killed the engine, she turned and leaned her face in close to mine, whispering, "Mom, I am this close." She gestured with her forefinger and thumb close together. "I can feel it. I just know it. Just trust me."

Hmm, well, good.

Jenna's Journal

April 18

> In case I don't make it back, I'd just like to say that I will always love everybody mentioned in this journal, and I'll be with you no matter what. I'm sorry to everybody I've wronged, and I thank everybody who's been kind, helpful, loving to me especially: my Mommy, Tom, Daddy, Nate, Greg, Jennifer, Marie, Kerri, Gabe, and anybody else I've forgotten.
>
> Please know that my hand will be on your shoulder while you're crying for me, and I will watch over you as best I can.
>
> Please don't forget me.

Wednesday and Thursday Jenna lay in a tiny heap on the sofa, trying to regather the little strength she could in time for the performance Thursday night. She barely made it to the show, but she made it. We were all there, even her father. Her play went smoothly, but Jenna looked positively ghastly. I was near tears the whole evening. What must people think? I had only to wait to find out. After the performances, the mother of one of Jenna's girlfriends, a busybody whose endless interfering, albeit well-intentioned, phone calls always left me more upset, strode up to me after the show and had to remark how horrible Jenna looked and how "concerned" she was.

"Maybe if I bring her some of my homemade chicken soup? Everybody loves it."

Oh, yeah, Marilyn, that'll do it; she's only been starving herself to suicide because no food could attract her like your fucking CHICKEN SOUP, I wanted to scream. I knew she meant well, I knew she spoke from the blunder of ignorance, but I wanted to slap her face. I make good soup too, damn it.

I collapsed into bed that night completely exhausted from the emotions of the evening, the week, the year.

Jenna's Journal

April 19

I am teetering on the edge of something here and I don't know what to do. Yesterday wasn't perfect, it wasn't fantastic, but it was a lot better than the past few weeks. I tried really hard all day and had a nice dinner with Mom at night… but then had two bowls of cereal before bed. Then (now here's the terrible and strange part) this morning in 7-Eleven I just took a donut and ate it in line.

Right there. Then, as if that weren't enough, after I paid for my water, I headed back and stole a muffin. I just opened the little plexi-glass door and pulled it out, left the store as if it were mine. I've been reduced to theft, here, people! And I couldn't have just taken a bagel, either. It had to be this huge, fattening banana-nut thing. And I ate it. And enjoyed it. And didn't do it to satisfy a hunger. I'm just so sick. Ugh. I'm just so…scared, too.

April 21

I became violently ill after a day of bingeing on Monday. Then had a strangely simultaneously horrible yesterday when Mom stayed home to take care of me and took me to the doctor. Later we talked… a lot… and took a nice bike ride together.

I feel as though I am at an important crossroads right now. I feel like I have to stop this disorder right now, or at last as soon as possible and stop waiting or else I am going to swing to the other side of the pendulum, which is something I can't afford to do.

Food is not directed at me—it does not have to be personified. I have to stop when I am full. I can live without this disorder. It will be okay.

I can and it will.

I can and it will.

I can and it will.

It's time to say goodbye.

APRIL 22

Sometimes at night, deep in the dark, I feel like my only friend is the clock radio beside my head. And even that must be turned off eventually. Then I am left with shadows and empty, outstretched arms reaching from the pit of my soul.

I am afraid of death.

So I must live.

And then it happened. It just happened.

Sometimes we have moments in life that seem to make time stop. Moments when we know that life has taken a sharp turn and will never be the same. I'd like to say that I knew at that moment that Jenna was miraculously healed. The truth is, I did not. But Jenna did. I do not use the word *epiphany* lightly or carelessly, but that describes the next event in my daughter's life - an earth-shattering, life-altering moment of clarity and enlightenment. I just didn't know it at the time.

It came the next night, Friday, April 23. Jenna was determined to attend a drama club dance at school, despite the week she had had. She got home late that night, came into our bedroom and woke me up.

"Mom, Mom, I have something to show you. You have to see this!"

Groggy, I turned on my bedside light.

"Watch," she said. She held up a pair of scissors, then cut off the braided friendship bracelet from Willow Creek six months earlier. I flashed back to her announcing she'd wear it till it fell off by itself. Now, she stood next to my bed and proudly cut the damn thing off. A tiny act it was, but I suspect somewhere on the other side of the planet, the earth shook in response. I was afraid to read too much into it at the time, but I believe God's hand was on hers at that moment.

She said, "Go back to sleep for now; we'll talk tomorrow and I'll tell you all about it. And Mommy, I love you from the ground to God, you know."

With that, the vanquished demon piteously slinked out our back door into the April night, humiliated to have been defeated by an eighteen-year-old, sixty-four-pound weakling.

Shhh--shh--be very quiet. be very still. write very small so no one will hear. whisper this so the gods less loving do not know—my baby is being healed.

The next morning, Jenna-Marie rose unusually early. I was sitting at the breakfast table, enjoying the calm of a Saturday morning before the rest of the family was up, mulling over my girl's strange visit the night before. As she came downstairs and into the kitchen, she seemed to walk differently. Sitting down next to me, she poured herself a cup of coffee. With cream.

"Today is the day, Mom. I am throwing this off me. I want to live. I am missing out on too much of life. I am going to start eating meals with all of you again." Her words were bubbling over themselves. "I want to food shop with you, not alone. I've decided I *am* ready. I am changed, starting today. I am back and I've missed you."

I leaned across to her and took her hand, "Dearest, you haven't missed me; I've been here. You've missed yourself."

"Yes, well, Jenna's back," she said with a smile.

My daughter glowed. She carried a look different than I had seen in her in ten months.

"Well, carry on," I told her. Inside, I thought, *"we'll see."* I was not ready to hope. *I'll smile later*, I thought. *I'll exhale much later.*

That weekend she talked and talked and talked. I listened. And watched very closely. "I feel like an Eskimo who's been curled up, fetal-like, under a heavy fur skin blanket. I am throwing it off in this grand gesture, see? I throw it off, this Thing. I have been so disconnected from my body."

"But what made this happen?" I asked.

She leaned back in her chair with a physical ease I hadn't seen in a long time. She thought for a moment, as if wanting to get this right. "When I walked into the dance last night, Marie offered me a chocolate-chip cookie and it bothered me so much. Then all of a sudden, I realized that there would be so many special events coming up in the next couple of months, with the drama club banquet, and the senior breakfast, and graduation, and they would all involve food. Everything does."

"That's because food is the ultimate celebration; it's the giving and sustaining of life itself."

"Well," she went on, "I decided I don't want to miss out on so many moments in life, and I don't want to dread them all because of food. I want to live."

My puny brain was having trouble processing all of this.

"And Mom, you know that friendship bracelet? It started out as a gesture of my friendship with Audrey, but it became a symbol for my eating disorder. It was a sign of my sickness. And I didn't want to let it go. Remember that day when you kept wanting me to take it off 'cause it had gotten so dirty and grody? You kept saying, 'Take it off; it's disgusting!' And I said, 'No!'" She was laughing. "Well, that bracelet was kind of like a companion for me. So last night I had to show you that

I was serious in the only way I could. I had to cut it off so it couldn't be put back on again."

It wasn't her words that struck me; talk is cheap. It was just her Self. It is in the eyes, the poets say. Her eyes were no longer muddy-colored, dead and empty-looking. They had their old sparkle and vividness back, a rich deep brown. Her smile emanated from somewhere deep inside her, a sort of wakefulness. Her very breath reached deeper into her lungs, every word filled with serenity and spirit. It was my Jenna speaking for the first time in almost a year, not the demon, not the negative mind.

Jenna's Journal

April 27

just a quick waltz with me,
here in the bare
dewy green grass
just one little light
hop
and
a sweet little skip
along the cool wet blades
waving and laughing in the wind
twirl
and delight
and dance
with me.

Still, I was justifiably skeptical. I'm sure many afflicted with this disease will often pronounce to themselves and others their new-found resolve to slay their demon, only to fail, and watch their fingers lose their grip from around its throat, as it once again overpowers them. I did not rush to spread the good news, not even to my mother, who waited in daily expectation for a phone call that any progress had been made. I couldn't bear false hopes, and knew she could even less. If this was real, the evidence would clearly be seen soon enough in weight gain. It's that simple. I wanted to believe so badly. Gradually, I simply chose to believe, with a tiny lingering voice inside of me still saying, "We'll see, we'll see."

Chapter Twelve

Transcendence

And we did.

From that moment on, my daughter had, indeed, changed. It was not a slow uphill struggle; she simply ate with ease. The demon seemed to have left her body and soul as quickly as it had occupied it. Of course I watched her oh, so closely. *Is she eating, but now purging? Is she eating in front of me, but not any other time? Is this metamorphosis all going to collapse on top of itself in a day or two, a week or two? Oh God, don't make us fools.* Her eating seemed effortless and normal, as if there were no internal fight going on.

But this isn't really about food, is it? Eating is where we play out our feelings, the primary one being a desire to survive. It is where we use our power to sustain, nourish, starve, or stuff our souls. And it is in Jenna's soul that her healing was manifested. Simply said, she was back, in all her effervescent grab of life. Every cell of her being awoke. Her body responded quickly and noticeably to all around her. First, the eyes. Where vacant pools of dingy brown once stagnated, now her eyes seemed to peel away a cataract film of hopelessness, and dance with clarity and shine. Her skin changed from an almost transparent yellow to a healthy, rosy hue within days, as muscles, veins, organs all greedily responded to nourishment. Her bones gained strength, and she once again stood straight and firm. Jenna's brittle, thinning hair seemed to mend overnight, thickening and taking on a luster as before. To watch this Dorian Gray reversal was remarkable. The body really does not ask so much of us, just attention, and it will love us back one hundred fold.

Jenna's Journal

April 30

> Right at this moment, life is so lovely. It's a beautiful feeling not to be in the mood to write depressing poetry.
>
> It's such a freedom I've been feeling… I am liberated.

It was only after a couple of weeks into the transformation we had been witnessing at home that I finally, tentatively, confided to my mother what was happening. She said, "Honey, you must feel like a great burden has been lifted off your shoulders."

"Not entirely," I told her. "It's more like I have been trying to breathe with a huge pile of heavy stones on me. So with every step of recovery, with every bite she eats, another stone is lifted, another heavy rock off my chest, back, head, heart, legs; I feel it everywhere."

Each day held the same trepidation, but a little less. Each mealtime held the same anxiety, but a little less.

My love notes to Jenna continued. I was rewarded with hers in return.

"Dearest, dearest Mom, Each time I see a little love letter waiting for me, I know I'll be going to sleep happy. Your words float and dance about inside my heart and weave a web of sweetness and light around it, giving it a protective structure, strength, and warmth that I happily nestle into, and my lips reach up and up and up... into a sentimental, tear-filled, happy smile. I love you from the ground to God. And I love knowing that you love me. Jenna-pie."

Readjusting back to "normal" came easy for us all. Jenna's depression had vanished, her view of life restored. With energy bordering on euphoria, she plunged herself in to her fun high school events and now even juggled two jobs successfully. She no longer slept away her weekends, and her coping skills in handling life's bumps seemed stable and sound.

From the outside, I saw the healing in her face. She was smiling again. How we take for granted the sincere smile that is so much more than the muscles which lie around the lips. Eyes bright. Laugh ready. I knew that those lucky enough to be in Jenna's world those early days would notice her progress for themselves. Inwardly and outwardly, her health showed itself quickly to all those around her.

We often keep silent out of fear and confusion when those around us begin to not look quite right. What does one say, after all? "Gee, you're looking really bad these days. Are you sick? Is it catching? Should I even be talking to you?" But words come easier when we have something good to say. At school, Jenna's peers, teachers, and administrators alike were quick to notice and mention her rapid return to health. Jenna was reinforced every day by those around her. Several students, some whom she barely knew, felt compelled to tell her, "You're looking really good these days." Some did not even quite know how or why, adding, "What's changed about you?" She would just smile and shrug. And come home to tell me.

"Mom, today a boy I barely know came up to me and said, 'You look different.' He looked at me kind of weird. I just said, 'A lot of people have been telling me that lately.' Then he said, 'Your facial structure is different or something. You look really pretty.' Pretty. It's been so long since someone has called me pretty and I believed it. But this time I actually did. And that was a good feeling. It's nice to have people staring at me for a positive reason. I'm slowly learning how to honor my body; I appreciate it and respect it."

Can this really be happening? Oddly, I returned to that inevitable *Why*, only now from the other side of the coin.

Just one week into her recovery, Jenna came home from school and proudly announced, "I'm going to prom!" At the last minute she had asked a friend in her drama class who, as a sophomore, was probably bowled over to be asked at all. *Way to go, sweetie.* I wanted to cry with joy, not because prom is so important, but that it is part of the everyday chapters of experience for a normal high school senior. For me, it meant that Jenna was back in the moment.

Prom was in five days, so the hunt was suddenly on for a dress that would complement her still abnormal form. Although her physical progress was not lost on anyone, recovery is gradual, and she had far from an attractive, healthy look. We both knew it would not be easy to find the right formal ensemble. Most styles are revealing, with backless scooped necks and spaghetti straps, and while I knew how important it was not to deny her recent struggle, I wanted to help make this Cinderella feel beautiful for a night.

Standing in the communal dressing room of the small formal-wear shop in the mall, she tried on gown after gown. The shop owner was a tiny woman in her sixties with a Middle Eastern accent and abrasive manner whose approach with every girl in there was to aggressively try to sell everything from tiaras to rhinestone buckles. However, she handled Jenna and me with dignity and sensitivity. Looking at my daughter, she understood her special fashion needs, and guided her toward complementing designs that didn't scream, "Hey I've been really sick for months!" in a dorky way. I was a little worried that in Jenna's new realization of things, she would see how unhealthy she still looked and be plunged back into a depression. Or she would be clueless and choose a frock that emphasized her still-emaciated appearance. A few weeks earlier, she literally would not have been able to see the extent of her physical deterioration. Instead, her perspective now was accurate, balanced, a clue that her thinking had truly changed. She acknowledged and accepted the ravages of her disease that still remained; she no longer denied or minimized the reality of what reflected back to her in the mirror. She knew that she did not look well yet, and accepted that fact with uncommon grace, patiently smiling through the whole affair. After all, she was going to prom!

Finally we found something that made her feel beautiful: a lovely garnet-colored, chiffon A-line with a sheer yoke that ended in a high collar band of velvet with a matching velvet cape. In a way, this sophisticated, yet modest, prom dress was the beginning outward sign of Jenna's returning shape, a self-definition of sorts.

David showed up at our house the next Saturday night to take our daughter to her first and only prom. Being only fifteen himself, his older sister served as taxi driver. As they posed for pictures, I had to stifle a bit of a giggle at the sight. David was as coffee black as Jenna was alabaster white. He was half her height, yet she probably weighed even less than he. Two years younger, he had the expectant glow of a heady sophomore having been asked out by an older woman.

Jenna beamed.

David remains a good friend today. I still giggle at the prom pictures.

Jenna's Journal

May 21

There is a soul within me
growing and growing each moment
inside.
Her voice
Her song
must be heard
She will sing one day
and the world
will hear
her.

Just as Jenna's outward appearance recovered, so did her exterior environment—her room. After a long year of self-deprivation of every kind, Jenna began to direct eye and energy to decorating her bedroom. I kept all unsolicited suggestions to myself, sensing she must see this blank palette as her arena for self-expression. First, she bought an assortment of reproductions of her favorite art classics and hung them all around the room. Beauty and masterpiece. Next she wrote little phrases of inspiration and taped them everywhere. She asked if she could paint actual words or designs on the walls. Hell, she could have asked for a sequined ceiling and the answer would have been yes! I was thrilled to see her giving a darn about anything, and her room was her room. If I had learned anything in the past year, it was what the entrees in life were, and what were the side dishes. Inconsequentials could be seen for what they were. "Sure, hon. Have some fun with this," I smiled.

She painted D-R-E-A-M above her closet with curlicues and filigrees in deep reds and blues. She pasted recent inspirational cards from loving friends and family all over her closet doors. She lined her dresser mirror with photos of good times, hung a humble straw cross over her bed, and posted *No Bad Karma* over her door.

Jenna was re-emerging.

As if in her own twelve-step program, she knew she needed to make peace with her friends - friends who, with the Pollyanna loyalty of teenagers, had earlier sent her notes of encouragement and get-well cards, or asked her to join them in high school activities, but then drifted to the background when she had answered them cruelly, or not at all. One at a time, she called, wrote to, or sat down with each one to express an honest apology for any hurt she had caused them, and to ask for their hands back in friendship. In our Catholic faith, the act of reconciliation is a sacrament, and here, too, was a sacred exchange of spirit, to be sure. Every single one of these young people welcomed her back with the generous blessing of reconciliation.

"Mom," Jenna spurted out as she came through the door one day after school, "Marie cried when I talked with her today. She kept hugging me so hard. I had been so afraid to approach her, but it was as if none of this ever happened, and she said she was just so happy to have me back!"

"I am so glad to hear that, Hon!"

"You know, it's true that you find out who your friends are when something bad happens and the fake ones desert you, but these weeks I've found that the real friends, the ones who also notice when something very good happens without you telling them, they comment on it."

I smiled as she continued, curled up in my arms as we sat on the sofa.

"And in a few weeks, I going to be ending a huge part of my life and starting a new one. It's kinda scary. The trick, I think, is to learn how to take the good stuff from the first part and carry it to the next. Mommy, thank you. You have held me and been my strength when I had none. I will always need you. I will always love you. I will always, always thank God for you."

We sat in silence for a long moment. It was such a different silence than so many times before.

Shhh...be very quiet when giving thanks. Be quiet and still.

Jenna's Journal

May 22

> I shall wear a hat on my graduation day, and toss it high and far above my head into freedom and the world and the warm mid-evening sky. I shall wear a hat while I huddle close to someone dear and count down 3... 2... 1... Happy New Year in Times Square. I shall wear a hat as I stroll down an uphill lane in San Francisco and wear bobby pins and hope it doesn't blow away in the late afternoon wind. I shall wear a hat and hold it in place as I bend down and pick up my little dog to save her from the puddle created by the Seattle rain outside our apartment. I shall wear a hat as I linger and wander among Paris's finest art galleries, discussing the real reason Miss Mona

> Lisa is smirking so secretively. I shall wear a hat as I part my mouth into a posed, but genuine smile and await the click of the camera as I stand just on the edge of a cliff in Ireland. And I shall wear a hat when I'm a little old lady, walking down the street or sitting on my porch or making senseless conversation with the cashier in the grocery store or playing cards with my little old lady friends… until one day someone will hang up my hats for me… or hopefully put one of them on her own head.

Jenna graduated with her class in May, and as she coasted through the summer, college was fast approaching. In the end, she opted to attend nearby Arizona State University, but still wanted to live in the dorm. While I was grateful she would be much closer to home, I knew that, away from my watchful, knowing eyes, she could still slip so easily back down into the well of ill. But at least she would be only twenty minutes away. I knew I needed to show enough trust in her to let her go, give her space to become. How hard that can be.

Parenting is all about giving away. Kahil Gibran offers the piercing revelation that, "Your children are not your children… Though they are with you, yet they belong not to you.." Birth is not really a receiving, but a letting go. We let go at birth. We let go at weaning. We let go when first grade rolls around, and the first sleepover, and grandma's for the summer. We let go with that driver's license, first date, and graduation, and finally another's hand in marriage. We'd better learn early how to open our own arms and hands and release our little doves to the universe. Sometimes we can't even see it coming.

I had to let go on that day in the doctor's parking lot. It was time, I knew, to let go again.

Jenna's Journal

July 28

I am so indescribably happy.

I am finally really overcoming this.

I sometimes have the urge to get rid of all of my journals of when I had my disorder, because if something happened to me, and someone like my mom found it and read it, I think she would cry and be disappointed and wish she could have done something (which she couldn't have). Because as much as I insisted that it was never a weight issue, I look back and read what I wrote about feeling guilty. But I really believe that it wasn't me writing, not my soul. It was like it was a different person. Some demon taking over me.

So, Mom, or anybody else who should read this, please realize that, in logic, I did know that I was deathly skeletal, and I never in my heart really felt fat. Please believe me.

I love you.

My daughter and I dove into the delightfully mundane tasks of preparing to move in to a college dormitory, shopping for odd-size bed linens, a bulletin board, laundry bag, microwave oven and a used bike. Checking out the room and finding out storage is woefully inadequate. Meeting your dorm mate and discovering she's into horses and the NBA, and you are not. You know, all the things college kids do. But every day felt like a gift from God for me. Before I knew it, though, the time had come. The night before she left for college, Jenna lay on my bed with me for over an hour—not curled fetal in my arms in the dark, but on her belly, head propped on her elbows—as she shared her anticipation over her upcoming new life.

She seemed to want, to *need* to talk about It, recapture it all. Last summer, Willow Creek, the leg motion, how she'd look at her hands and perceive them as healthy-looking as they now were, instead of the reality. She couldn't see how bad it was then. She talked about her psychotic terror the night she came home from Willow Creek, terrified she was going to die. Of how overwhelmed she still was that her friends didn't desert her. Of what she was trying to learn from this and her coping skills. Of her concern for Timmy at Willow Creek, that he was doing so poorly when she left, and she wondered if he was all right.

As she spoke, my own memories of hospital visits, Ensure™, her depression, my midnight walks on the golf course alone in winter, phone calls during class, interfering acquaintances, friends' awkwardness, all flooded back.

Jenna's speech was bubbly and indescribably normal. I gazed at her bright eyes, round curves and sharp senses, but I winced inside. *I cannot talk about this dark time as readily as you can*, I wanted to tell her. She was enjoying a newly healed soul and body, that euphoria pumping in, like coming out of having the flu for five days. I still had the deep concern of a mother. I could not yet comfortably reminisce with "Boy, weren't those days something...," giggling at how "crazy" it all was. After all, the demon could be in the bushes listening, waiting for a vulnerable time to return.

It was all too fresh; recovery was too new. I was still too close to tears because I was, am, the mother. Maybe Jenna always knew she'd come out of this, as she said. But I didn't. I had been in a place she could never understand, and it was still a breath away - the pain, the possibility.

I wanted to plead with her, *Please don't keep reliving this. I can't go there yet.* But I didn't. I listened patiently, suspecting that she needed to talk about it, to process it all. In silence I just marveled at her recovery and ability to discuss her experience.

Jenna's Journal

August 8

Dear God,

Please, please help me through this transitional period in my life. Please walk with me, help me let go of friends who are leaving, accept new friends into my life, and be kind to those who need friends as much as I do. Please help me to live healthfully and wisely. Please help me to keep my head above the chaos and make it through. Please ease my fears and allow joy, love, and learning into my life. And please help me find my classes. I love you. Thank you for everything you've blessed me with thus far. Good night.

Moving day finally came, and I felt the full range of sentiments, from pride to excitement to the inevitable maternal pangs of separation. The last few months had been a blessed reunion of familial spirit in our house. We were all getting reacquainted, almost falling in new love with one another, the five of us. Nate and Greg were gradually trusting their sister's return to health, and all three were delicately weaving together their own threads of reconciliation. To have her now leave for the campus of ASU seemed a painful passage indeed. God, how I would miss her daily presence. I also stifled nagging thoughts that we might grow apart. Would I see her often enough to know if she wasn't eating? Can she make it on her own?

Then there was the secret part of me that, frankly, looked forward to my caretaking shift being put on a shelf. I had to have a break; I needed to not be so needed. I needed to not live day-to-day with the person who can blink wrong and set my mother anxiety mode into highest gear. I didn't want her to leave, yet I needed her to leave. I was eager to finally establish a stable home life in which each member wasn't living on the edge. Tom, especially, had earned this.

These tugs of emotion couldn't sort themselves out; each just looped itself through my mind and body, colliding with the other. So while Tom, Greg, Jenna, and I drove in tandem with nearly all my little girl's belongings, I followed close behind Jenna on the freeway, and fought back tears all the way. Mustn't let her see me cry. Mustn't worry her. I am Mother. I can do this too, and this is a day for joy.

As I stood in the doorway of Sahuaro Hall at Arizona State University, holding my daughter in a tight embrace, my mind flashed back to a mere ten months earlier when we two stood in another residential hall filled with other young adults. This time my sense of security came from locks on the inside, not the outside.

Chapter Thirteen

Metamorphosis

It is remarkable how rapidly the body responds to recovery. It is designed to survive and thrive. With even a bit of nurturing, it will answer you positively. It wants to be well. It is meant to be well. It rewards.

I asked Jenna, "How are you feeling, really? Is it a struggle? Is it a daily effort?"

"No," she giggled, "It's no effort. It's simply gone!"

We all began to exhale.

"And Jenna, is she still eating?" my mother cautiously asked now and then.

"Yes, she is, Mom."

For some time the pain of this year welled up in my throat. I still wanted to keep Jenna's progress to a whisper, wondering if I would ever breathe in deep enough. My questions were quieter, but there. Why did she fall victim? Why did it leave so suddenly? What are we to learn from this? How are we to have changed? Was this simply her deciding to be done, or did we feel the lift of God's hand under us?

I had been to the blackest hole a mother can face without falling in. I was the privileged.

Once at college, Jenna's body repaired itself quickly. She was still adjusting to a new eating lifestyle while, like every other college freshman, trying to adapt to new freedoms, routines, and expectations. She ate heartily. Quite soon she recovered the weight she'd lost and then some. Of course, I never uttered a comment regarding her appearance, but when she'd see recent photos of herself, it was clear how uncomfortable she was with this equally unfamiliar reflection. She was desperately ready to redefine herself, to mold a new look in clothes and hair to match the constantly shifting self in the mirror, but she wasn't sure who that self now was.

Jenna's Journal

September 12

This morning when I was parting my hair, I noticed that I had tons and tons of little baby hairs sprouting from the top of my head. I was sort of bummed, because I thought I looked like a weirdo.

Then, this afternoon at home, Mom was patting my hair and said, "Why do you have all these little hairs here?" And then I think we both thought the same thing at the same time, because we simultaneously smiled and she said what I was thinking, "They're the hairs you lost, growing back."

So now I don't mind them so much.

Plus, the jeans that I used to wear to bed that would often easily slide off my hips to the ground before I could even make it from my bed to the bathroom next door, now fit snugly around my waist.

One afternoon she came over to look at magazines, trying to pick out a new hairstyle. Suddenly she dropped her head down in tears.

She cried, "I wish last year had never happened. When I see myself, I don't know who I am. This new weight doesn't matter to me, but I don't see myself that way. I don't see myself like last year, either. My self-image is as I was in my junior year of high school before everything happened. I don't know who I am, so how can I pick out the right hairstyle for *me?*"

"Jenna, some never recover from this disorder. Most do, but they do so through slow, painstaking process. I can imagine how your spontaneous new health must be hard to absorb."

"Yeah," she interjected, "I wish I hadn't healed so quickly and completely. I wish my recovery was little by little."

"Don't you ever say that!" I scolded. "For those who endure years of suffering, this becomes a daily battle for them, a constant struggle to defeat their demons, just like any addiction. Your healing came the way it was supposed to for you. Do not *ever* envy those for whom this takes years. You were not as in charge of your recovery as you think. Yes, you decided to end this, but don't you think millions of sufferers go through periods of similar resolve? You didn't do this alone. You had to reach that point of determination, but I have no doubt of God's hand in your moment of healing. So do not question *how*. Be grateful for *is*."

She nodded. "I never do anything halfway. This disease was either going to kill me or I'd get over it just like that; there'd be no languishing and yo-yoing for years and years. I know my body is just trying to adjust to changes again, but I just don't know how to take them, how to see myself."

Sitting down next to me, she now began to sob, head on my lap.

"Jenna, I think it's a combination of physical, emotional and psychological behavior. Physically, your body is grabbing and holding on to everything you give it. It doesn't want to be starved again; this is its response. You're eating much more and with pleasure because, for one thing, you are making up for such devastating denial of want for a whole year. You denied yourself the indulgence of so many satisfying foods for so long, and you don't want to deny yourself any longer. And maybe you really are hungry, in a delayed way.

"But we are both doing a lot of speculating. You need to talk to someone, you need information. You should research and find out what to be expecting when total and complete recovery from an eating disorder happens, because you are not alone. Others do experience this. We both just need to understand more than we do now. Why not call Dr. Singer at Willow Creek?"

"Oh, I liked him."

"Good. Call him and sit down and talk with him about what you're going through. It could be that it will take your body as long to regulate itself as it took to nearly destroy itself. It might even take longer. It could be that you need a well-designed food plan during this adjustment. But information is empowering, no?"

"Yes," she returned with a smile.

Jenna visited Dr. Singer the following week. He was stunned to meet my daughter, essentially for the first time. *Yes, this is Jenna. You don't know her. Someone took her body's place for a time. But this is really her. See the light in those deep brown eyes, hear the lilt in her voice? Feel her ebullient spirit and love of life? This is my beautiful child.* He did not even recognize her.

Dr. Singer told Jenna that, yes, some patients suddenly, and somewhat mysteriously, escape from anorexia's clutches, but it is rare. She is very lucky. He also reassured her that the body's response is as individual as the disease itself. Everyone heals at his or her own pace and form. She must have patience in working with her body to find its settling point.

Jenna seemed better able to handle her recovery after this. In fact, when I announced to her that I would be participating in Phoenix's annual charity Walk for AIDS, she asked, "Can I do it with you?"

I had lost a close friend and colleague to AIDS five years earlier, and this seemed a tiny, but positive, way to pay honor to his memory. Like hundreds of other people touched by Steve's life, my daughter, too, had adored him, and I was so pleased that she and I would walk together to increase understanding, and halt the ravaging power of his merciless executioner.

It was only seven months into Jenna's recovery, and already she looked healthy, normal, downright fit, so I kept quiet the voice inside that questioned if she was hardy enough for the six mile trek through the streets of downtown Phoenix. *Trust, trust.*

"Sure, honey, that would be terrific."

Arriving at Phoenix Civic Plaza on a crisp Sunday morning in November, with $476 dollars in pledges we had raised at our schools, we looked around at an ocean of love. Thousands of caring men, women and children, most of whose lives had been punctured by this disease at close range, assembled with a paradoxical peaceful solemnity that the optimism of proaction brings with it. We are not totally helpless; there are things we can do. I thought back to the sorrow when we lost Steve, and it was a reminder for us both that eating disorders aren't the only despicable curses on the earth.

The day's event proved to be a perfect time for mother and daughter to really talk. Feeling a strange sense of intimacy in the middle of a constantly flowing human river of ten thousand others, we walked fast and slow, deliberate and meandering. Among all these strangers, we shared the energy of friendship and alliance as streams of walkers carried on lively conversations and even shared a laugh now and then. Of course Jen and I spoke of Steve, whose love of life, laughter, friends and teaching touched so many others, and what a damned loss for all to see him succumb at age forty-two. We talked about college, family, local news events and kept the chatter going as it helped each mile pass more easily.

Then as we hit Mile 4, the tone abruptly changed. Walkers entered a section of a city park lined with staked paper tulips of all colors labeled with names of AIDS victims, along with placards asking for our reverent silence through this mile of garden, and inviting each to reflect on why we were here. Footsteps slowed. Voices became mute. This impromptu community of social militants turned into a procession of mourners. Weeping could be heard.

As we emerged from this tunnel of grief, my dialogue with Jenna turned serious and thick with purpose, as we began to dissect the year we had just survived. I decided to simply ask her why she had become anorexic, having avoided the actual question ever since the onset of her recovery. I suppose I figured the distraction of our walk in public daylight would deflect some of the discomfort of such a poignant topic. And the sobriety of the mile we had just walked made small talk seem grossly out of place. Still, it seemed a bit bizarre to confront such a raw subject so spontaneously. So I was surprised by her apparent comfort in honestly discussing it, intellectually, with no leaps into any emotional crevices.

"I don't know, Mom. I think I had just outgrown everything. My friends suddenly seemed so immature and silly. And school seemed so irrelevant. I just was done, in my mind. I was ready to move on, yet I was stuck for another whole year. I didn't think I could stand it. I no longer fit in with the world I had always loved. It depressed me. I just wanted out of everything that was teenaged. I felt like I couldn't breathe, and I couldn't explain that logically to anyone."

"But why starve yourself? How could this be a solution?"

"I don't know."

"Did you want to die?"

"Not really. No. No, I didn't. I just wanted to leave my life. You know, it's funny, I feel more in control now that I don't care how much control I have. Does that make sense?"

"I guess, in a way."

We walked in silence for another mile. Even as I thought over what she had tried to explain to me, I felt myself clinging to my own theory in contrast - that rather than her having matured too suddenly, I believed she feared growing up. She was so close to her mother, so involved and successful in school, so happy in life as it was, that her senior year looming signaled a quickly approaching end to all that she has known. Eating means nourishment, nourishment means growth. We grow up and away, and that can be a frightening prospect. Physically, anorexia halts normal development; menses stop, for example. It is almost like the body is saying, *Halt! Wait for my mind to catch up. Time must freeze until I am ready.* While she was sick, she took on some very childlike behaviors, and it just didn't ring logical for me that all of this was because she was so ready to be adult.

But I accepted what she was telling me now, stayed private with my own amateur psychology, and remembered the counselors' cautioning us that we may never know the true origin of this, and that's O.K.

It was like something was in her water for a year. Then it wasn't.

"Jenna, all I know is, I see how well you're adjusting to college life. You are healthy, you are learning, and you're making it on your own. That's all that matters in the end, eh?"

"Yea, Mommy. And I love you, love you, love you for being there," she sang as she wrapped her strong arm around my waist and grinned.

"And I always will be, baby. From the ground to God."

When I dropped her off back at her dorm room, Jenna looked at me with sad eyes and said, "Mom, remember Audrey from Willow Creek, the one with the spiky short red hair?"

I remembered. By red, she meant like red dye #8 for M & M's. She was a quiet, lonely waif who seemed to rely on extreme or alternative ways of being heard. Audrey was also Jenna's friendship-bracelet buddy. I nodded, "Yes, I do."

"When I visited Willow Creek, I found out she died recently."

"Oh, I'm so sorry to hear that. How did she die?" I stupidly asked, slipping into a naïve sense that all was right with everyone else's world now, too.

Jenna gave me an odd look as if to say, *don't you know?* then mumbled, "Well, anorexia, Mom."

A chill. And an overwhelming blanket of sadness. My body gave a shudder and later, with no one around, I wept. I wept for Audrey and every other person, young and old, male and female, who goes into battle against this vile disease, and loses.

It lies right below the uppermost layer of my skin. One tiny shred of thought and I am there, I am back there feeling the grief and terror in the bowels of my heart just as if it were in my present. Will it always be like this?

Jenna's Journal

October 1

I am realizing the power and beauty and forgiveness of life. I have been a terrible person, especially in my illness. I have lied to the ones I love the most, I have stolen, I have manipulated those closest to my heart and people who were trying to help me. I have isolated myself, alienated my soul from the world. I have hurt and offended and confused so many people who didn't deserve it. I have ignored people who loved and cared for me, I ignored my body, controlled and manipulated my body, and nearly destroyed my body. I threw away (or put aside) everything I knew about nutrition, emotional well-being and unconditional love. Although I did not stop believing in God and trusting Him, my prayers and relationship with Him became impassionate and unfamiliar. I nearly killed myself, body and soul.

And yet, I survived. And now I am in college and trying to give my life feasible direction and make myself a better person. I will always be sorry for what I did, how I acted, the way I treated people and myself. But I have been given another chance, and I will embrace it.

October 15

Today as I was riding my bike back to the dorm from English class, I noticed a figure ahead of me. I didn't think much of her until I noticed how her pants fit. Although she was small (and so were the jeans) they seemed very baggy on her. At first I thought that might just be her style—oversized clothes. I started to think back to when my clothes were baggy, and I remembered that they fit me just like hers were fitting: no form whatsoever. I didn't think about it much until I realized that in addition to heavy jeans, she was wearing a warm, bulky sweater on top. Naturally this seemed odd to me since it's 103° and I'm dying of the heat. That's when the warning bells went off. Instantly, I remembered how utterly cold I used to get, even when no one else was.

As I rode past her, I didn't want to make her feel like anyone was staring at her. I remember how people would just gaze at me and think I didn't notice… but I did. I could feel their eyes on me. But I didn't want her to feel that way, at least not on account of me. So I barely glanced at her out of the corner of my eye as I went by. As I thought it might be, her face was drawn, her cheeks very sunken, jaw practically undefined. Her eyes were lowered and there was a fair amount of fine hair on her upper lip, and wisps of hair bordering her forehead. The small portion of her hands that were visible from her sweatshirt were bony, skeletal, and looked like they shouldn't be bearing the burden of the books they carried.

Her walk was slow and lonely. I felt so sad as I rode away.

All night I've been thinking about her and saying to myself, "Why didn't I stop?" But what could I have possibly said to her?

I know better than anyone that if you have that sickness, you will not get better completely, or fully accept anyone's help unless you want it.

OCTOBER 16

Why can't people see just how beautiful they are? How come people complain of their tiny imperfections, when in reality none of it really matters? Why can't we just see and acknowledge and appreciate and believe in the features, inside and out, that are unique and lovely? Why can't we just take that and go into the world, confident in who and what we all are naturally? How come we never realize our own individual splendor until it's too late and we're looking at old pictures of ourselves, marveling at our own and others' beauty? Why do we so rarely just recognize and enjoy our selves and all that we give to one another?

NOVEMBER 29

I am sitting on the floor of my bedroom at home. The smell of the heater drops into and occupies random spots of air. It is the eve of Thanksgiving and I do have much to be grateful for, indeed. Today was a gloriously cool one. The leaves fiercely clinging to the trees are a brilliant, alive shade of green. I am healthy (relatively speaking). I am surrounded by people whom I love and who love me, people who make me laugh and appreciate this gift some call Life. I am not without problems… I often have flashes of complete insecurity. But they pass and in the end mean nothing, simply what I believe to be the residue of old bad habits. But I am broken of those habits.

I cannot possibly ever name everything that I am grateful for.

DECEMBER 31

My maturation
has been
interrupted,
Switched all around
Wise at twelve
Paused
Held back at seventeen
Insecure and naïve
At nineteen
Awake and yet confused
Different
Always.

Starting with a moment of true epiphany on an April night, Jenna confidently stepped forward, never to look back. As she reached her first year of healing, she exuded health and vitality. Her strong arms would firmly grab my own body in frequent and ready hugs. Most of all, she was embracing life. She and I often enjoyed going out to lunch, where she ate with enthusiasm. "Umm, ooh, yum, let's have a brownie sundae!" she'd giggle as she picked out dessert. I was awe-struck.

The most important tool a human has is language. And yet, so often when we need it most, it fails us. How many times and in how many ways can I thank my God for the great force of healing? I reach down inside for words and all that come up are tears. Maybe that is the language. Maybe the soul speaks what the brain cannot. God must speak this language. I've always believed that there is no such thing as tears of joy; they are merely out of the relief in the absence of sorrow.

I'm not sure what my concept of God is. It tends to run tailor-made for me, far from the constructs of my Catholic upbringing or any other religion. But I am convinced of a tremendous Spirit whose force is loving and knows all that should and is to be. In a way, I believe in a Mother God, a giver of Life, who embraces us in time of need, washing over us all that is natural, and who hears the pleas of all mothers here on earth. How can I begin to know the magnificent language fitting to thank the divine benefactor? Words fail.

For me, the most beautiful concept from my catechism teachings is that of grace. It is God's blessing with no strings attached. A gift. Not because we've asked for it, or even earned it, because we usually haven't. It is the ultimate bestowment. Just the pure giving that is love.

The grace of God quietly, softly struck our family. I worked hard to believe my daughter's dramatic declaration that April night, and she was right.

One the first anniversary of her recovery, Jenna slipped another love note on my pillow. It read,

> *What is the point to life? There is no "point." We must laugh. We must think. We must dance. We must sing. We must s-t-r-e-t-c-h. We must reach.*

> *We must cry. We must jump up and down! We must look up at the blue and stare at the clouds and see shapes in them. We must write. We must speak. We must communicate. We must learn. We must teach. We must experiment. We must experience. We must be scared. We must be brave. We must let our hearts love and be loved and let them be broken and mend them together and let them love again. We must be vulnerable. We must try. We must embrace each other and ourselves and the earth below us and the world around us and the life within us. We must change. We must see art and read poetry and stories and listen to music. We must help each other. We must be full of color. We must cherish what we've been given and strive for what we want. We must spend time alone. We must spend time together. We must forgive each other and ourselves. We must be honest to each other and ourselves. We must follow the passion that lies within us and drives us forward. We must breathe. We must create. We must dream. We must believe. We must live.*

My Jenna was starting to live again.

Epilogue

Today, Jenna is living magnificently.

As she made her way through college, I watched a young woman thrive in that euphoria of *after-illness*. Post-starvation chubbiness gave way to a comfortable body shape. She now looks about the way I would have predicted through the first seventeen years of her life. More importantly, she has found a life balance, with no obvious remnants from *the year*, at least that I can see. We don't mention the experience very often, but she seems at peace with it when it finds its way into talk.

Her first summer of recovery, she visited her great-Uncle Matt in New Jersey for two weeks. He took her under his grandfatherly wing as they shared a love for New York City, jazz, and life. Her second summer, she landed a job in West Virginia as a camp counselor for girls, and managed to live without a hair dryer and make-up for three months. Her third summer she traveled to Italy for a six-week study in Italian and art history. The other side of the world! I accepted each of these adventures with a mother's unease.

My own parents raised me to think that the living room was called that because that's where one does one's living. When at age forty I announced that I was fulfilling a lifelong dream to visit Ireland, they had a fit. "Why would you want to do that?" they asked. "But we will worry so much about you!" They just didn't understand. But I did. And I understood my daughter. She needed to go; she needed to fly. She'd be back.

So I watched her take baby steps, then giant ones. Her identity took shape as she realized that she belonged anywhere she found herself. For a couple of years, that belonging was in Paris, where she discovered that one of her favorite things about her beloved City of Light was the food!

Jenna is now an accomplished writer and lives in Manhattan, her second favorite place to live. She moves through city streets with the ease of one who knows herself.

Does she have moments of faltering, and fearing the monster's return - even courting it? I can't know. Will she ever relapse? Maybe. Statistics reveal a fairly high rate within the first five years. Will I ever totally exhale thinking of Jenna? I will always look at her in a closer way. Does she look a little thinner? Is she losing weight? How is her eating? Is she stable emotionally? Is she well in spirit? What do her eyes say to me? Am I saying the right or wrong things? What were the triggers leading up to her illness? *Are* there triggers today? I will never assume her wellness; that security, while a false one, was taken from me forever. When I am eighty and my girl is fifty-one, we may sit together sharing coffee and conversation, and I will be looking, wondering, hoping, trusting, loving. And remembering. Just under the skin, fear of the demon lies.

But with each passing year, all of these concerns hold less and less power over me, less and less space in my brain.

Living with a life-threatening illness changes everyone in the household. And once one has been threatened by death, it puts life itself into sharper perspective. What might be monumental issues to others more easily distracted by minutia, are seen for the trivialities they are. When Jenna makes life decisions I do not agree with, or behaves in ways of which I do not approve, I am pulled back from a possible sharp rebuke, reminding myself that at least she is alive and healthy. How could I want for anything more? This has helped me to maintain a balanced perspective on what is most important in life.

Looking back on our year of sloshing through the dangerous, murky waters of a critical illness, I came to a surprising realization. Crisis comes with a bizarre residue, a sort of cream that rises to the top. Strangely, I never felt more alive, more awake, more in the moment of each day than during that year. It was as if every pore were enlarged and open, every nerve sat on the surface of my skin, raw and vulnerable to the elements. Everyone's words were louder, every detail in a room was exaggerated. My life was a day at a time, an hour at a time. Every minute was crucial; therefore, each second became larger than life. Each present moment demanded that I be in it.

It was also the year that I felt the closest to my daughter. She demanded so much of my time, thought, and emotional energy. Yes, the world revolved around Jenna; it just had to for awhile. The rest of us simply needed to accept that and place things second until a healthier time. This girl seemed to roll a normal kid's share of grief and turmoil into one year. *O.K., we can all help.*

In the doing, she and I became inextricably bound to each other, even at the ugliest times. She was my little helpless girl again; she needed her mommy. And while I knew this wasn't normal and it wasn't healthy, it was what she needed, for whatever reason. I tried not to judge it. I would be there for her. I would rock her in my arms forever.

It was a raw time of living for me, for all of us. It was a year for self-examination, for a test of one's faith, for the strange power, even freedom, that comes from total helplessness. Truly, it is in the letting go that we gain the most control. In a sea of strangers I found myself thinking, *None of you knows what is behind my facade. None of you knows what I am going through at this moment!* Then I would think, *What are you facing today that I don't know about?* We go through our routines, we go to work, run errands, pay the bills, say "please" and "thank you" and keep the house clean. And all the while, we may be clutched in threatening whirlpools of pain and fear. *What will tomorrow bring?*

As all families do, we now compartmentalize this period in our little family's history for the sake of household conversation. "Before or after *the accident*, or *the divorce*, or *the move*, or *the, you know, event*," whatever it happens to be. We refer to it as "when Jenna was sick," or The Year. It helps us gauge our own family timeline and remind us of its past tense. Every year on April twenty-third, I send my daughter a little card or leave her a phone message, just reminding her how much I love her. I never mention the significance of the timing, but she knows.

"Mom, I got your message. Thanks. It means a lot to me, especially this week."

More need not be said.

Despite any of my own theories, I still see the arrival and departure of anorexia as a mystery. For us, the demon came, nearly killed, and left. Today, too many children and adolescents, along with women and men of all ages, fall victim, up to twenty percent of whom will die in its grip. The majority of the remaining battle it for years upon years, suffering a multitude of permanent dysfunctions and physical damage, some eventually recovering completely, others dying suddenly from heart failure or other organ shutdowns after too many years of self-abuse as the body steadily deteriorates. Not really surprising, as one is in a race against oneself and against time. It is gradual suicide.

An anorexic's world is a lonely and misunderstood one. We must acknowledge that it is actually not an *eating* disorder, but a *mental* disorder, and thereby complex, and exacerbated by bias and misunderstanding. The most powerful weapon is early and professional intervention, but many do not receive it.

Like anything else she puts her mind to, my overachieving daughter excelled in anorexia nervosa. Jenna was a poster child for all its ugly descriptions, quickly mastering a fast track to an early death. My family doctor continues to shake his head in disbelief.

"Valerie," he says each time I give him an update, "this just does not happen. As bad as she was when I saw her, this total and sudden recovery is quite remarkable." But, in fact, recovery can be sudden, and Jenna is its testament.

As for me, I have become somewhat of the token mother-survivor of eating disorders in my limited universe. Soon after my experience, I became close to one of my students who, after taking my eleventh grade honors English class, became my classroom aide. One day I learned she was becoming self-abusive through anorexia, bulimia, and even self-mutilation. She knew about my experience and felt comfortable revealing her struggles to me. Through the years since, we have become close friends. As I have watched her move in and out of treatment programs, continuing the battle to this day, I see her slowly winning the war.

It's funny how the strings of synchronicity are orchestrated to bring people together. Many times a friend or colleague has asked me to talk with a mother in a similar situation. I am aware that I am comfortable to do this only because my story has a happy ending. I get to speak of healing. Mostly, I just listen. Only those who have lived through such an isolating journey know better than to slip into conventional assumptions or condemnations. To the many parents I talk with and groups I speak to, I feel a bond, as if we are all members of an invisible club where confusion and fear rule. I give these fellow seekers my own story to hold on to. But all mothers and fathers and children must walk their own paths.

Recently, I came in to the teacher's lounge to find a fellow teacher sitting alone at a long work table. A physical education teacher, whose path didn't cross mine often in a school with a staff of a hundred and thirty, I didn't know her well, but I liked her. She gave me a half-smile as I crossed the room to fill my coffee cup. Ordinarily during a hectic prep period, I would have just dashed in and out, but something compelled me to take a moment and sit down to say with all sincerity, "Good morning, Angela. How are you?"

She must have sensed that I didn't mean it as the usual mindless greeting.

"Well," she spoke tentatively, "not so good." *Gee, Angela, don't you know a rhetorical question when you hear one?* I wanted to joke. But I didn't. She then went on to tell me all about her daughter who had just been placed in out-of-town residential treatment for anorexia. Like my daughter, hers was seventeen and a half. Like my daughter, hers was about to be a high school senior. Like me, this mother didn't understand this insidious malady and didn't know what to do. Like me, she was hanging on at work by that thread that keeps us going. Like me, her eyes brimmed with tears as she found uncommon intimacy with someone she hardly knew.

I listened for some time, hoping my face transmitted concern and familiarity, no shock or fear, or worse, recrimination. I thought she must be sharing her deepest troubles with me because she had heard I had been through it.

"No," she said, with a look of surprise when I asked. "Actually," she continued, "during church last Sunday, the minister was talking about how we don't really let people into our lives. People say, 'How are you?' and we always just say, 'Fine,' when clearly we are not! When you asked me just now how I was, I thought of that and decided to take a chance and actually tell you. I had no idea you had been through this, too!"

I smiled, held her hand, and told her all I could in a short time. "Angela, I am here for you. I get to tell you that there's hope."

During the first Christmas season of our family's healing, Jenna, Tom, Greg, and I attended a play at the Galvin Playhouse where Jenna worked in the box office on A.S.U. campus. What a rare treat to be spending a Saturday evening together at the theatre. Jenna was elated just being out with her family. During the play, she rummaged through her bag to find some gum and instead pulled out a small item, turned to me with a smile, and opened her hand. Sitting there in her palm, was the small azure stone with *HOPE* engraved in gold. Jenna smiled at me as we wrapped arms around each other, I clutching to my hope, my daughter, Jenna-Marie.

And this is why I write my story. Because where there is one miracle, there is another. Where one parent and child fought down the demon, another pair may. Maya Angelou reminds us that, "A bird doesn't sing because it has an answer; it sings because it has a song." I do not have answers; I offer no solutions. Only hope. But sometimes hope alone gets us through, helps us rise in the morning, gather strength to wrap around a firm purpose. Hope allows us to look into the eyes of those in despair as we offer hands, arms, smiles of understanding, or at least acceptance. *If her child won, maybe mine will, too.* Hope is the armament, love the weapon, to penetrate the horrific shell and reach the inherent, loving spirit within.

Hate the demon; love the child.

Today is Easter Sunday. As I sit out on our deck this morning writing this, the sun rises, and a cool baptismal breeze washes over my face. All the archetypical symbolism is not lost on this foolish poet. Sentimental stuff. But today marks another springtime re-birthday for Jenna, and I will give my daughter one last plain stone in her favorite dark red color, carved in the shape of a heart.

All the rest of the world is hers.

Love Letters to Jenna

~ No. 1 ~

A love letter to my daughter

First in a series…

Dear Jenna-Marie,

Such joy as I have never known, the day you were born. A daughter! I have a daughter! At that moment, I fell in love with you—not for anything you said or did, or would say or do; just for your very presence. I love the fact that you exist – that you're here—that you are a child of the universe.

You need not *ever* earn my love; it is yours! Forever. Unconditionally. With total acceptance. You will never be without it. I am your mother and I am here for you.

M.

~ No. 2 ~

"I see your true colors shining through
I see your true colors that's why I love you
So don't be afraid to let them show.
Your true colors, true colors, true colors are Beautiful
Like a rainbow..."

M.

~ No. 3 ~

Dear Jenna,

Lately, when I think of you, I keep thinking the word "fabric." I realize the intricacy of the fibers that we are each woven from. Threads from our experiences, our thoughts—every color a different hue, some fibers tough and coarse, some delicate and fine. Bolts of yarn are dull on the shelf, but when woven together, beautiful complex patterns emerge. Every single thread is important, crucial to the strength and endurance of the piece.

My darling daughter, every fiber of your being is a vital color that makes you unique and valued and loved.

One fiber is your love of language and poetry.

So, how did you like my metaphors tonight?

I love you,

M.

~ No. 4 ~

Dearest Daughter,

As I've been carefully tearing each of these pages out with an aim for precision and clean, straight lines, I have felt a pang of dismay as each sheet tore ragged, haphazard. Then I realized, that's part of the fun, the unpredictability. Each comes out different and interesting. I am learning to write within the space I am given.

How *perfect* is imperfection!

M.

~ No. 5 ~

Dearest Daughter,

Know this:

You are, in time, place, and spirit, where you are *supposed* to be. Right *now*. Grab it! Use it! Learn from it! This moment is precious and so are *you*.

The difficult moments will pass, but they are meant to be explored first.

What a valuable growth experience this is for us all…

You will be all right tomorrow. I know it. God's loving hands are all around you.

I love you.

We love you.

You love you.

M.

(One from Tom—)

Jenna,

We appreciate all the hard work you do all week in all your roles. It is a tremendous lot to ask of someone; it doesn't go unnoticed.

Those who love you must ask you to continue the hard work *for yourself.* They are standing by making available all they have to help you. Please continue to use their help.

Everyone *still* wishes the very best for you. They are confident that you will realize the long, full, healthy life you deserve.

Make peace with yourself and all your healers and helpers.

We love you, and our lives are greatly enriched by you.

Tom

~ No. 6 ~

Dearest Daughter,

My love letter to you comes from Marianne Williamson, and later shared by Nelson Mandela.

Love, Mom

"Our deepest fear is not that we are inadequate.
Our deepest fear is that
We are powerful beyond measure.
It is our light, not our darkness,
That most frightens us.
We ask ourselves, who am I to be brilliant,
Gorgeous, talented and fabulous?
You are a Child of God.
Your playing small doesn't serve the world.
There's nothing enlightened about shrinking so that
Other people won't feel insecure around you.
We were born to make manifest
The glory of God that is within us.
It's not just in some of us; it's in everyone.
And as we let our own light shine,
we unconsciously give other people
Permission to do the same.
As we are liberated from our own fears,
our presence automatically liberates others."

~ No. 7 ~

Dearest Daughter,

I LOVE YOU.
I SHALL NOT ABANDON YOU.

Mother

~ No. 8 ~

Dearest Daughter,

These things I know:

- That I love you. I love every fiber, cell, eyelash, toenail and lovely long fingers that are you.
- That I love you for your wit, compassion, poetic spirit that is you.
- That good will come of this experience.
- That I will never abandon you.
- That those in your presence are better off for it.
- That you have a special talented air about you that is needed here on Earth
- That you love me
- That God has an extraordinary life planned for you.
- That you know all of the above, too.

These things I believe:

- That you will recover fully.
- That your friends will never abandon you, nor you them.
- That your tremendous strength, courage and inner core wisdom will see us all through.

- That you want goodness, pleasure and happiness for your life.
- That you cherish God's love and life.
- That you believe all these, too.

Love, Mom.

~ No. 9 ~

Dearest Daughter,

My thoughts tonight are these:

I love you so completely, so thoroughly, so unconditionally. I know you know that. Now, know this—I think you are showing tremendous strength and resilience. I know how you are working hard on your recovery. I know you value your life. I see many tiny, yet monumental movements forward these days.

I cannot fully know what you're going through. You say I am the fighter—my dear daughter, look at you. I am humbled by your courage and spirit. I mean this so deeply. You are *my* role model!

Every step forward comes with effort and faith, and *is* rewarded.

God is laying His hands on you.

Love, Momma

~ No. 10 ~

Dearest Daughter,

We shared some wonderful laughter today in two movies. You have a most engaging smile that melts me! Your brown eyes twinkle; they really do.

You are transforming. You are healing. I see you carving out strength, patience, and will as you make your way through. Such powerful intelligence you bring to this. I am in awe of you.

Life truly is in the little moments—movies, rides in the car, cuddles, family meals, music shared.

This letter has no poetic theme to it. But I missed writing to you.

I am praying for you, too, tonight, honey. You have already succeeded!

Love always,

Mom

~ No. 11 ~

Dearest Daughter,

The young oak tree tries so hard to be firm and tough and rigid to brace itself against the storm. It snaps.

The young willow stays loose, bending to the currents of the winds. Its very flexibility strengthens it.

Be the willow.

Be the seashell that rolls and bobs up to shore with the tide, then lets the wave take it back again.

Be the supple leaf that gently drops upon the surface of the river's flow and lets the current move it along in rhythm with the water.

Be the grains of sand that abandoningly let winds roll them into new sculptures.

Learn your lessons from nature.

Hope does float. As do peace, and faith, and love, and trust.

Be the willow, my darling.

Love from your mother

~ No. 12 ~

Dearest Daughter,

Let every pore of your being open up. Open yourself and let the warm love all around you seep in. Let the positive voice of Self only speak to you. Let the love your brothers have for you be clear to you. Let your friends' love invite you in. Let the warm embrace of family hold you. Let the light of God's love sustain and nourish you.

For you are a Child of God and are so worthy. Listen to your needs, whatever they be, and love thy Self.

You are a beautiful creature—the time to live well is now.

I love you truly,

Your mother.

~ No. 13 ~

Dearest Daughter

Christmas Day, 1998—a love letter.

I love how strong you were today.

I love how joyfully giving you were today.

I love that you had good food.

I love my pearly candle.

I love how beautiful you looked in your champagne sweater.

I love your organized recycling!

I love that you went to your dad's.

I love my Beanie Baby, "Wrinkles." How utterly thoughtful.

I love your presence and presents.

I love the Jenna jewel box.

I love YOU!

Mother.

~ No. 14 ~

Dearest Daughter

New Year's Eve.

On this last day of the year, I wish you peace. I wish you love. I wish you strength. I wish you health. I wish you angels guiding your way. I wish you wisdom. I wish you safety. I wish you warmth. I wish you gentility.

Through all this difficult, challenging, confusing year, you have been blessed in receiving and bestowing all of the above.

God's watching over you, love.

I love my life because you're in it.

Happy NEW Year, Jenna-Marie.

Love,

Mother.

~ No. 15 ~

Dearest Daughter,

I love you through and through.

That is that.

Through good times and bad, arguments and embraces, distance and togetherness.

Your precious love for me is the second most vital thing to me. First is your health, well-being and happiness.

A mother's love is such that she would give up all, even her child's love and adoration, for that child's wellness. It's that simple and that complex.

I pray I needn't lose either.

I love you. Help me through this, too.

Love,

Mother.

~ No. 16 ~

Dearest Daughter,

You have made many wise choices these last few days, luv.

You are remarkable.

Each day is a reinvention.

Be strong.

All will be well.

All *will* be well.

Love, strength, and wisdom surround your decisions.

God's warm hand is on you.

I love you always and all ways,

Mother.

~ No. 17 ~

Dearest Daughter,

You have tremendous power.

I see power in your movements.

There is power in your smile.

I feel power in your touch.

I hear power in your speech.

I sense power in your thoughts.

You share the power of love with those who are in your heart.

Love is the ultimate power. Always use wisely. It is returned to you a hundred-fold.

I love you, dearest,

Mother.

~ No. 18 ~

Dearest Daughter,

"At the bottom of the abyss comes the voice of salvation. The black moment is the moment when the real message of transformation is going to come. At the darkest comes the light." Joseph Campbell.

I am grateful you are my daughter.

I thank my God for you.

Love,

Mother.

~ No. 19 ~

Dearest Daughter,

You're still beautiful. Your big brown eyes still twinkle when you smile warmly. Your long fingers are graceful in every gesture. You walk with such style. Your face and smooth skin are lovely yet. You will always be beautiful. Your inner beauty—that of love—comes through in your very being. Really.

Now, return to healthy.

I love you, I love you, I love you.

Mother.

~ No. 20 ~

To my daughter on the occasion of your eighteenth birthday

Dearest Jenna-Marie,

Each birthday is special, but this is an important one. Today looks like yesterday yet something is different. You are welcomed into the world again, now, as a young woman. Much has not changed; I am still your mother, you are still essential to our family. But the day marks the milestone that is *adult.*

I will always see in you the creamy, round face of my infant daughter with the big brown eyes. I will see dresses you've worn, "Bunny" and dolls you've cared for, dancing to Walt Disney movie tunes, a broken wrist, choral concerts, and teaching you to drive.

Now, the journey just flows on unfolding, blossoming; I look forward to it all! Cherish the child in you. Embrace the woman becoming. Both are exquisitely beautiful and valued. Remember the River: Lie back, float, and smile at those traveling alongside you. Be wise. Trust in God and your spiritual guides. Believe in yourself. Rely on Love. It is you.

Blessings of Peace on your 18th!

Love always, Mother

~ No. 21 ~

Dearest Daughter,

I wonder if you hear me in the next room as I tear this paper out and smile, knowing there's a love letter coming.

I wonder if you know how often I think of you during the day, how often I see you in the eyes of the girls who are my students.

I wonder if you know I look at a picture of you on my desk, speak to it and send you love.

I wonder if you know how many others send up prayers for your health.

I wonder if you know how closely I listen to you.

I wonder if you know how much I love you. Nah, you cannot.

Mother.

~ No. 22 ~

Dearest Daughter,

I like so many things about you.

I like how cheerful and loving you are every morning.

I like how you take risks.

I like how you take good advice.

I like how encouraging you are to those around you.

I like your sense of humor and ready laugh.

I like browsing in bookstores with you and talking movies.

I like your banana bread.

I like your warm wonderful personality.

I like your glowing presence.

It's been lovely having you home this week.

I like you. I love you!

Mums.

~ No. 23 ~

Dearest Daughter,

Lately I have noticed you have been wearing a lot of butterflies, on your clothes, your jewelry. How appropriate. You are going through exciting changes, stages, days and lessons. Some are painful, some fall light as rain on your face as you giggle in comprehension.

Today I saw another change in you. On the campus of A.S.U., you stood a little taller, more secure, and looking so expectantly happy.

You are daily adding colors to your wings, my girl, vibrant colors to strong wings flexing to take you soaring through your future.

You are beautiful.

I love you,

Mom.

~ No. 24 ~

Dearest Daughter,

Thank you, thank you for getting well.

Love and peace,
Mother

Acknowledgements

Writing is a solitary sport. During Jenna's illness, I turned to my closest friends: Pen and Paper. I wrote to keep sane, to steady my voice and quiet my nerves. I also sensed the importance of preserving the experience, regardless of its outcome. Wisdom sometimes waits to appear long after the moment.

But no book makes it into the hands of any reader without a village behind it.

After spending five years writing this book in secret, stealing early-dawn hours on Sunday mornings, it was time to tell Jenna. "I've written a book." "Mom, that's great!" "Uh, it's about the year of your being sick." "Oh. Wow. Well, I kept a journal through it all. If you think it would add anything, you're welcome to use it."

Jenna-Marie Warnecke's help on this book was invaluable. It started with her bravery in sharing her most private thoughts, and continued all the way to her being a most brilliant and brutal editor. A talented writer herself, she held me to high standards, particularly reminding me of Stephen King's (and others') admonition to "kill your darlings" in pursuit of concise language. I'm still working on that. Jenna, I love you from the ground to God.

I owe much to my mother, Loretta Beatrice Scharf Stapleton, who taught me, by example, the profound depths of a mother's love.

Daniela Rapp, senior editor at St. Martin's Press, was the first to believe in the value of this story, and worked hard to see it in print. Her painstaking editing and professional endorsement kept me going.

I am indebted to early readers, Joanie Judd, Dr. Rhonda McDonnell, Barbara Curry, and Dr. David Bernstein, who handled my literary baby with tenderness, encouragement, and valuable suggestions.

I thank Dr. Bianca Bernstein, Professor of Counseling and Counseling Psychology in the College of Letters and Science at Arizona State University, Tempe AZ, who thrust me in to speaking in public about Jenna's and my experience. Her graduate students have been waiting a long time to see this story in print.

To my friend, Brenda Bradfield Calhoun, thank you for prodding me through the years with, "Valerie, when is that book coming out? People need it!"

To the mothers and fathers I've met who have begged to read our family's story for the hope it offers them.

I thank the staff and doctors associated with Willow Creek for their selfless work to break the vicious stranglehold of eating disorders that threatens so many patients.

I am grateful for my friendship with Cassie Consten Sampson, who shared valuable resources with me. She understands, fights the fight, and serves as a light of inspiration and courage in sharing her own world. When teacher and student become life-long friends, it's a special thing.

My sincerest thanks go to Emily Groeber, editor-extraordinaire, who makes anything I write, better!

I am very fortunate to have been divinely guided to Netanel Miles-Yépez (Albion-Andalus Books): writer, artist, teacher, and publisher of my first book, *The Risk of Sorrow*. For the second time, he has recognized the worth of my writing and that of a story that serves the greater good.

I thank editorial assistant, Samantha Krezinski, for her tireless editing, correcting, and invaluable support of this book.

My deep gratitude goes to my sister, Marsha Stapleton Sturla, who is always and forever there for me.

I thank my two wonderful sons, Nathan Warnecke and Gregory Warnecke, for keeping a steady course through our year from hell, loving Jenna and me through it all. I am so proud of the men they have become.

Lastly, I give my undying love, admiration, and appreciation to my husband, Tom who, on the day he married me, committed himself to all four of us. Every day, his strength, supreme patience, and unconditional love continue to sustain our family.

Suggested Reading

The Hungry Self by Kim Chernin

The Secret Language of Eating Disorders by Peggy Claude-Pierre

Reviving Ophelia by Mary Pipher

Feminist Perspectives on Eating Disorders by Patricia Fallon and Melanie Katzman

The Body Project: An Intimate History of American Girls by Joan Jacobs Brumberg

Eating by the Light of the Moon by Anita Johnston

Appetites by Caroline Knapp

About Valerie and Jenna

Photo by Tom Foster

Valerie Stapleton Foster is an educator, public speaker, and the author of *The Risk of Sorrow: Conversations with Holocaust Survivor, Helen Handler*, as well as a short story, "Loss," which was published in the *River Poets Anthology*. A recipient of the Shofar Zakhor award for Holocaust education, Valerie taught writing and literature for thirty years and currently holds an adjunct faculty position at Chandler-Gilbert Community College in Arizona, teaching future teachers. She lives in Gilbert, AZ with her husband, Tom, and may be reached at valeriefoster2016@gmail.com.

Jenna Warnecke is a poet, essayist, and fiction writer whose work has appeared or is forthcoming in *Kindred* and the *Washington*

Made in the USA
San Bernardino, CA
07 October 2017